THE ENCYCLOPEDIA OF
QUILTING
AND PATCHWORK
TECHNIQUES

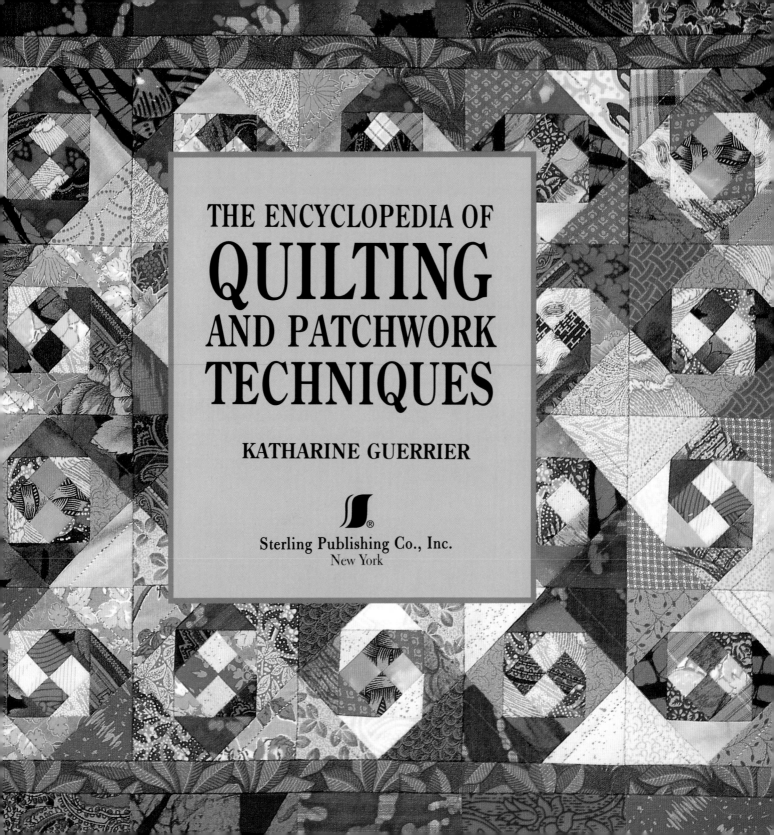

THE ENCYCLOPEDIA OF
QUILTING
AND PATCHWORK
TECHNIQUES

KATHARINE GUERRIER

Sterling Publishing Co., Inc.
New York

Conceived, designed, and produced by
Quarto Publishing plc
The Old Brewery
6 Blundell Street
London N7 9BH

Senior editor Honor Head
Editors Maggi McCormick, Catherine Bradley
Senior art editor Amanda Bakhtiar
Designer Sheila Volpe
Photographer Chas Wilder
Picture researcher Susannah Jayes
Picture manager Rebecca Horsewood

Art Director Moira Clinch
Publisher Piers Spence

Library of Congress Cataloging-in-Publication Data is available upon request

10 9 8 7 6 5 4 3 2

Published in 2002 by Sterling Publishing Co., Inc
387 Park Avenue South
New York
NY 10016-8810

Distributed in Canada by Sterling Publishing
c/o Canadian Manda Group
One Atlantic Avenue, Suite 105
Toronto, Ontario, Canada, M6K 3E7

Manufactured by Eray Scan Pte. Ltd., Singapore
Printed by Star Standard Industries Pte. Ltd., Sinapore

ISBN 0-8069-8907-6

Title verso quilt by Katharine Guerrier

CONTENTS

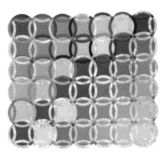

INTRODUCTION

FROM A CRAFT BORN OF NECESSITY QUILTMAKING HAS PROGRESSED TO A HIGHLY DECORATIVE ART FORM. THE COMBINATION OF PATCHWORK, APPLIQUÉ AND QUILTING WHICH TOGETHER MAKE UP THIS VERSATILE CRAFT AFFORDS IT GREAT POTENTIAL AS A MEDIUM FOR SELF-EXPRESSION. THIS RECOMMENDS IT TO QUILTMAKERS EXPERIMENTING ON ALL LEVELS, FROM SIMPLE TRADITIONAL DESIGNS TO ELABORATE INVESTIGATIONS OF COLOR AND PATTERN, AND WITH A WIDE RANGE OF MOTIVES, FROM DECORATING THE HOME, COMMEMORATING A SPECIAL EVENT, RAISING MONEY FOR CHARITY OR CREATING A WORK OF ART. THE MATERIALS AND EQUIPMENT REQUIRED ARE EASILY OBTAINABLE AND RELATIVELY CHEAP – IN SOME CASES EVEN RECYCLABLE FROM OTHER SEWING PROJECTS. ALTHOUGH THERE ARE NOW SPECIALTY STORES SELLING A WIDE RANGE OF EQUIPMENT FOR THE QUILTMAKER, A BEGINNER NEEDS ONLY THE BASICS TO MAKE A START: FABRICS, A SEWING KIT AND SOME TOOLS FOR DRAWING AND MAKING TEMPLATES.

Frederike Kohlhaussen
Korund
56 × 56 inches

ANATOMY OF THE QUILT

The craft of quiltmaking uses a range of technical terms to distinguish different parts of the quilt. Key aspects of this "anatomy" are illustrated opposite. It is important to remember that the quilt itself is basically a fabric sandwich consisting of three layers: the top (often covered with decorative patchwork or appliqué), the filler and the backing. The sandwich is held together by the quilting, which is often also an important decorative feature. The binding finishes the edges of the quilt to neaten and enclose the raw edges and filler.

It is worth pointing out the technical distinction between patchwork and appliqué. Patchwork, also known as piecing, is the technique of sewing small pieces of fabric together to create a large piece. Appliqué is the technique of cutting out pieces of fabric and stitching them to a background, usually to create a pictorial or representational design.

A quilt in progress, showing the **"Morning Star"** design. A freestanding quilting frame helps to keep the quilt taut over the area that is being worked.

Sashing or Lattice Strips A grid of fabric strips which can be used to separate out and to frame the blocks.

Blocks The design unit made from either patchwork or appliqué or a combination of the two repeated to make the quilt top. These can be set straight or "on point," that is diagonally so they form a diamond shape.

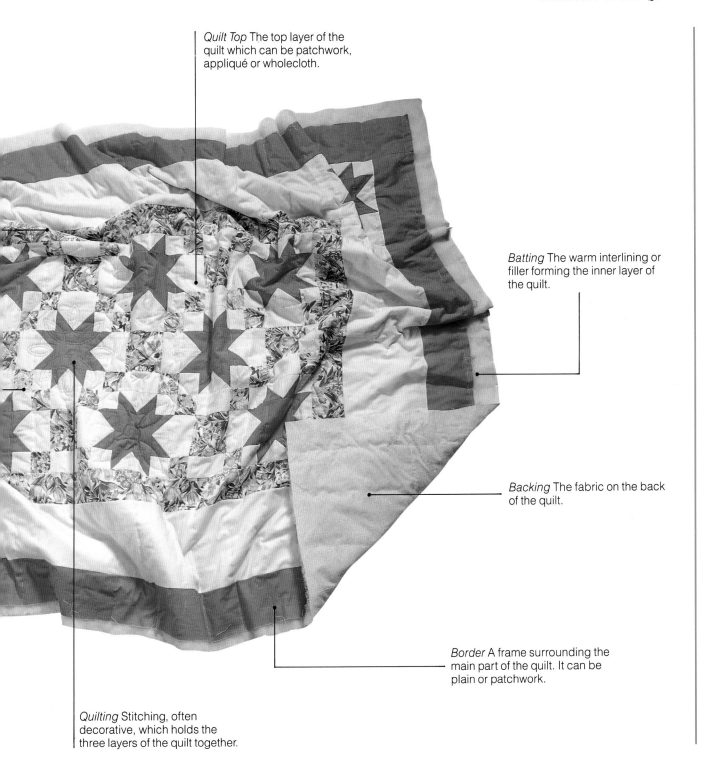

Quilt Top The top layer of the quilt which can be patchwork, appliqué or wholecloth.

Batting The warm interlining or filler forming the inner layer of the quilt.

Backing The fabric on the back of the quilt.

Border A frame surrounding the main part of the quilt. It can be plain or patchwork.

Quilting Stitching, often decorative, which holds the three layers of the quilt together.

1

5

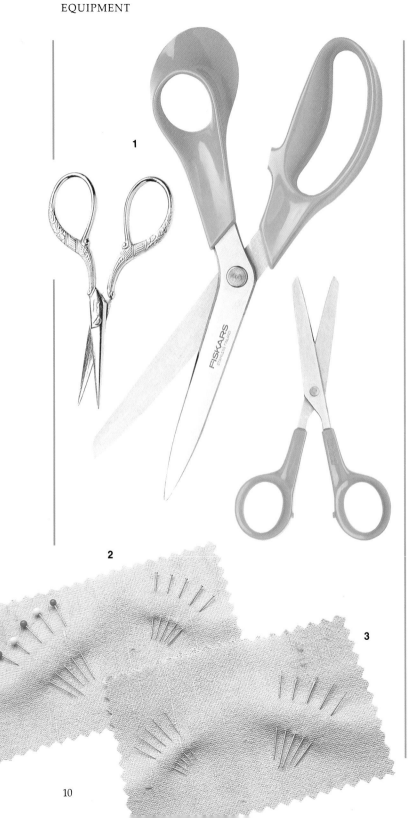

2

3

EQUIPMENT

You will probably already have many of the things necessary for making a start in patchwork and quilting. Have a look through your general sewing equipment before deciding what else you need. It is wise to buy the best quality tools and materials that you can afford, and if you are in doubt about making a choice when buying an expensive item like a new sewing machine, ask the advice of someone with experience, rather than being persuaded by an over-enthusiastic salesman. Patchwork was originally a craft of necessity and although today there is a whole industry devoted to supplying the needs of quilters, you can make a start with the basics and add to these as you progress, by which time you will have more idea of what will be useful and which products are just gimmicks.

The basic list of *equipment for cutting and sewing* should contain the following:

1 A top-quality pair of dressmaking scissors, a pair of paper-cutting scissors and a pair of fine embroidery scissors for trimming threads and seam allowances.

2 Glass-headed and wedding dress pins to cater for different thicknesses of fabric.

3 Hand-sewing needles, sharps no. 8 or 9 for general sewing and betweens no. 8 or 9 for quilting. The shorter needles have higher numbers.

4 Threads: a variety of colors for machine- and hand-sewing. A special thicker thread is available for hand-quilting.

5 Thimble: essential for hand-quilting and if you intend to hand-stitch patchwork. There are various designs of thimble especially for quilting, some metal with a flattened top, some plastic or leather.

6

12

4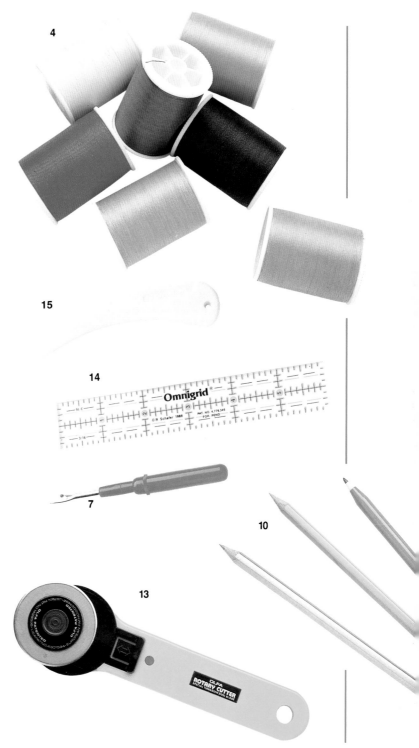

15

6 A beeswax cake prevents thread from knotting and strengthens it when hand-stitching.
7 Unpicker/seam ripper: useful for unpicking small stitches.
8 Steam iron for well-pressed patches and seams.
9 A sewing machine is essential for some types of patchwork, such as "Seminole" and "String" patchwork, and will speed up the process of construction in block patchwork.
10 Fabric marker: there are many on the market, find one which will draw a fine line.

11 Quilter's quarter: a small square plastic ruler ¼ inch thick on all sides. This is useful for checking seam allowances when making templates and stitching patches together.
12 Tape measure marked with small fractions.
13 Rotary-cutting set: this is optional but will speed up the cutting out process considerably (see page 40).
14 Omnigrid ruler for rotary cutting.
15 Hera marker, which leaves an indented groove on the fabric as an alternative to marker pen.

14

Omnigrid

10

7

11

13

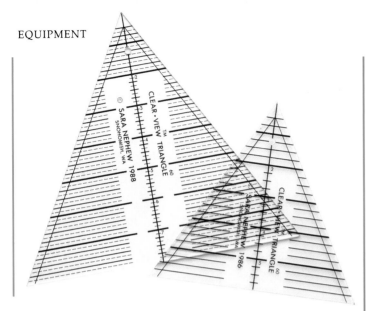

Templates and Stencils

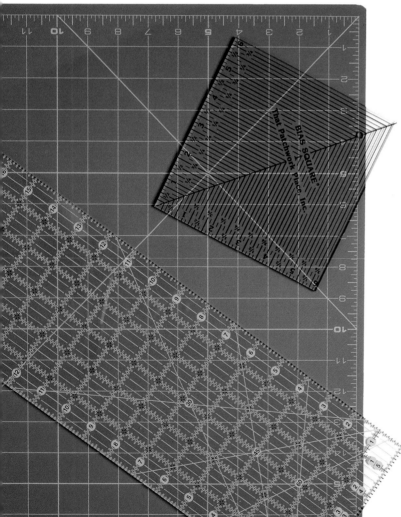

Templates and stencils are the master patterns for patchwork, appliqué and quilting. For *hand-stitched patchwork and appliqué* they are the finished size of the patch. As the fabric is cut, a seam allowance is added all round. There are many commercially available templates or you can make your own by drawing the block full size, cutting out one of each of the shapes necessary for the design and gluing them onto stiff cardboard or template plastic. When making your own templates, make every effort to be absolutely accurate; mistakes at this stage will affect subsequent processes. Use a fine pencil with a sharp point.

For pieced blocks, use graph paper to insure accuracy in drawing the angles. If seam allowance has been added to the template as for machine-pieced blocks, shapes can be drawn edge to edge on the fabric. When marking around templates onto fabric for either appliqué or pieced patchwork, choose a fabric marker with which you can make a fine line to maintain accuracy.

Where appropriate, mark the fabric grain line on templates. This should run vertically and horizontally through the blocks.

Templates for appliqué
These can be drawn freehand or traced from patterns. Make them from stiff cardboard or template plastic. Turnings are added as fabric is cut so the templates need to be the exact size and shape of the patch.

Templates for pieced patchwork
For hand-stitching a line is drawn all around these templates onto the wrong side of the fabric to act as a guideline when stitching the patches together. Seam allowance is added as the fabric is cut, so leave enough space between shapes to allow for this.

Templates for patchwork
For machine-stitching draw templates as for hand-stitching and mount them onto cardboard or plastic, then add ¼-inch seam allowance all round each piece before cutting them out. A quilter's quarter makes it easy to add the seam allowances. Mount the paper onto the base cardboard or plastic, then butt the quilter's quarter against the edges of the paper and draw a fine line all around to cut out on. This will give the correct seam allowance of ¼-inch.

Window templates

These enable you to frame a specific part of the fabric to position a motif. The inner shape is the finished patch size cut out to create a window. An outer frame of ¼ inch makes it possible to draw both the stitching and the cutting lines.

Where appropriate, mark the fabric grain line on templates. This should run vertically and horizontally through the blocks.

Quilting stencils

For elaborate quilting designs such as cables, shells and feathers, etc., you will need to use quilting stencils. These should be made of a durable material such as cardboard, plastic or metal.

When using the stencil, you need to mark carefully around the outside and through the channels cut in the templates. If the design is repeated, you need to indicate the position where it overlaps by making a dot or notch on the template. Keep the fabric marking pencil sharp to produce a fine line.

▲ A window template helps the quilter to place a design motif precisely in a patterned fabric.

Left, right and below. Examples of the different types of templates, stencils, and measuring tools available.

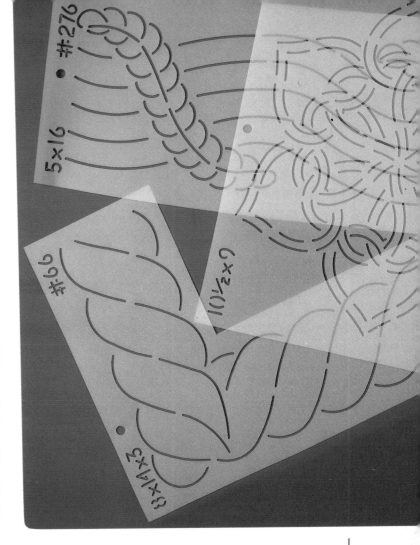

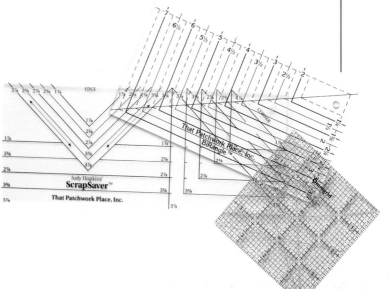

MATERIALS

Suitable fabrics for quiltmaking include pure cotton in dress or light furnishing weight, lawn, poplin and polycotton. Corduroy and needlecord can also be used, and their one-way pile or nap will give some interesting effects. Always wash fabrics separately before using them to shrink and test for dye fastness. If dye leaks out, continue to rinse until the water runs clear. If you are using old garments, cut away and discard any worn or faded parts. Avoid knitted fabrics as these will distort the fit of the patches and spoil the design. Exotic fabrics such as silk, velvet and taffeta can also be used, but may not be practical for items in everyday use – save these for decorative wallhangings and cushions which need less cleaning. A visit to a quilting supply store will demonstrate the wide range of plain and patterned fabrics available to the aspiring quiltmaker. Many stores also do mail order, some boasting over 1,000 prints and plains. Study the small ads in a needlework or quilting magazine. Apart from fabrics for the top, a quilt must also have a filler, the warm interlining known as batting and backing fabric to enclose it.

A range of fabrics
Different weights, different fibers, contrasting and complementary colors.

Small patterns can be matched with a plain color picking out one shade, or used together.

A trio of fabrics in different colors but similar tones.

Plain, geometric, and patterned fabrics may all be used together provided that shades are matched.

Backing
For hand-quilted pieces, choose soft cotton; sheeting can be used for machine-stitched quilts.

A range of batting
Various types of batting are available, each with different qualities and applications.

Batting

Batting is a very important part of the quilt and needs to be selected carefully. Many different materials are available to suit a quilt's purpose.

● *Polyester* This is a manmade fiber available in different thicknesses known by weight, 2 ounces being the thinnest and progressing to the thicker weights of 4 ounces, 6 ounces and 8 ounces. This is the most economical filler. Choose 2 ounces for stitched quilting; the thicker ones are easier to tie-quilt.

● *Cotton* This is available in two forms: pure cotton, which must be closely quilted or it will "migrate", that is move between the quilt top and backing and form lumps, and mixtures – one is called "Cotton Classic" – which contain some polyester and are easier to handle.

● *Domette* This is a woven interlining. It is used to give wallhangings a flatter look which makes them hang well.

● *Needlepunch* This is a polyester filler which has been flattened. Again, it is suitable for wallhangings.

● *Silk* This is used to give a quilt or garment a luxury feel. Rather expensive and perhaps best reserved for small projects using silk fabrics.

New products appear regularly so check the manufacturer's advertisements. Sometimes you will see the term "low loft" with regard to batting. This means that the batting is a flatter one which gives a less puffy appearance to the quilt.

● *Backing* The backing on a quilt is usually a whole piece of fabric although "Back Art" is a recent movement toward

making the back of the quilt worthy of attention. For a hand-quilted back choose soft cotton which will be easy to stitch through. Sheeting can be used for machine-quilting. Stitches will be less visible on patterned fabric than on plain. All fabrics used in a quilt should be similar in weight and fiber content. Using a thick, heavy fabric such as corduroy next to a fine lawn, for example, is not recommended.

WORKING
IT OUT

Once a decision has been made about the block designs to be used, you need to consider how you want to join the blocks. You should also think about using sashing or not, and whether you wish to add a border.

Stitching the blocks together edge to edge will create secondary designs, which appear between the blocks. These may be complex geometric patterns made by the shapes at the edges of the blocks merging together. Even seemingly simple blocks can have surprises in store when treated in this way. Lay out the blocks on a large, flat surface, and check that unwanted or unattractive secondary designs are not going to be created before joining them.

Blocks that need to be separated can be set apart with sashing strips. Sashing will also increase the size of the quilt top. Make a sketch of the quilt top with the number of blocks, sizes and the arrangement of the sashing strips to work out the necessary widths and lengths required.

Pieced borders must be designed and planned in the same way as the quilt blocks. Draw a section of the quilt to its actual size, with enough of the border to establish the required sizes of the pieces, and make templates if necessary. Piece the border and attach it to the sides, top and bottom of the quilt, matching points and corners where appropriate.

Group Quilts

A widely accepted and successful way of organizing a group quilt, or for an individual quilter to practice and learn many of the techniques of patchwork, appliqué, and quilting, is to make a sampler quilt. Each block is different, forming a visual catalog of designs. The blocks should be set with sashing strips to separate and frame them as in the example illustrated below. Blocks included in this quilt are (top row) 1. Sailboat; 2. Appliquéd church; 3. Flower medallion (second row) 4. Hawaiian sampler block; 5. Flower basket; 6. Jacob's ladder (third row) 7. A combination block containing Log Cabin, Star, Grandmother's Flower Garden, and Dresden Plate; 8. Weeping Willow; 9. Cathedral Window (fourth row) 10. Appliquéd poppy; 11. Crayons; 12. A mixed pieced and appliquéd block. The sashing strips are set with corner squares, and the quilting is done in a chevron pattern. The title brief *Quilting through the Century* evidently provided the members of the group who made the quilt with an opportunity to display their particular strengths.

Patchwork blocks

Patchwork blocks all essentially break down into smaller units, i.e., four-patch, nine-patch etc. Many blocks have traditionally been made as 12-inch blocks since 12 is divisible by 3 and 4. It is advisable to choose a block size that has the same ease of divisibility. Many people working patchwork by hand mark the sewing line and then judge the seam allowance by eye, but if you intend to use a sewing machine, an accurate cutting line including all seam allowances must be made.

Fairfield Processing Corp.
Group quilt
Quilting Through the Century.
65 × 80 inches

Estimating fabric

1 Make a sketch design of the entire quilt on graph paper with the correct number of blocks, and any sashing strips and borders required.

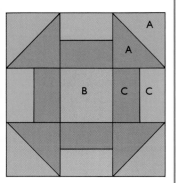

2 Decide on the number of different fabrics to be used in the blocks and draw a detailed plan of one block to indicate which fabrics will go where.

3 Count how many pieces of each shape will be required for one block. Multiply these totals by the number of blocks in the quilt to give the number of pieces needed overall in each different fabric and shape.

Measure the width of each type of fabric to be used and deduct 2 inches to account for the selvedge. Work out how many pieces can be cut across the width. Divide the complete number of pieces needed in a particular fabric by the number that can be cut from each width of the fabric and multiply the depth of the template by the answer. Round up this last figure to the nearest ¼ yard to estimate the amount of this type of fabric needed.

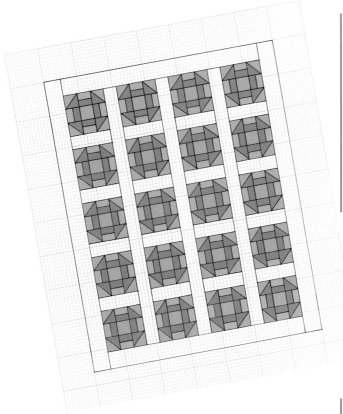

	I Block	20 Blocks
A (triangles)	4	80
C (rectangles)	4	80
A (triangles)	4	80
B (squares)	1	20
C (rectangles)	4	80

4 For the sashing, look at the sketch design, and count the number of strips required. For example, in the chart on the left, 19 sashing strips are needed, 16 horizontal and 3 vertical. Work out their length and width. Repeat the calculation for the four strips – two for the width and two for the depth – to make up the borders. Add 2 inches to the depth for seam allowance and estimate yardage required for both sashing and borders. It is important that sashing and borders are cut on the lengthwise grain of the fabric.

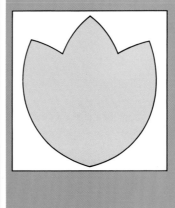

For appliqué templates, calculate to the nearest geometric shape. It is sensible to buy extra yardage to allow for mistakes; if it is not used for the intended project, it can be saved and built up into a collection for future scrap quilts and smaller items.

TECHNIQUES

ALTHOUGH PATCHWORK AND QUILTING HAVE THEIR ORIGINS IN ECONOMY AND THRIFT, THEIR DECORATIVE ASPECTS HAVE ALWAYS BEEN ACKNOWLEDGED. THE VERSATILITY OF PATCHWORK AND QUILTING LIES TO A GREAT EXTENT IN THE VARIETY OF TECHNIQUES THAT COMPRISE THE CRAFT. THIS SECTION DISCUSSES PROJECTS SUITABLE FOR ALL LEVELS OF ABILITY, FROM SIMPLE PIECED BLOCK DESIGNS FOR THE BEGINNER EXPERIMENTING WITH COLOR, PATTERN AND TEXTURE TO MORE COMPLEX CHALLENGES FOR THE EXPERIENCED NEEDLEWORKER. AS SKILLS AND CONFIDENCE INCREASE WITH PRACTICE, IT WILL BECOME CLEAR THAT THE DIVERSE FABRICS AND STITCHING TECHNIQUES PRESENTED HERE CAN PROVIDE A FASCINATING OPPORTUNITY TO EXPRESS INDIVIDUAL CREATIVITY. BOTH THE TRADITIONAL TECHNIQUES, SUCH AS "ENGLISH" OR MOSAIC PATCHWORK, BLOCK PATCHWORK AND APPLIQUE, AND MORE RECENT DEVELOPMENTS USING ROTARY CUTTERS AND SEWING MACHINES ARE CONSIDERED IN THE FOLLOWING PAGES.

Natalia Manley
The Fabric of Life is Burning
56 × 60 inches

BLOCKS

Blocks consist of a repeated unit of shapes which, when stitched together, form the basis of a quilt design. From early beginnings when simple one-patch patterns involving squares, rectangles or diamonds made full use of scrap bag fabrics, designs were invented and refined, often by folding paper into four or nine equal divisions of a square, then subdividing the resulting grid into further geometric shapes – smaller squares, triangles or rhomboids. This formed the basis of block design. Although originally brought from Europe, it was explored and extended by American quilters who made it uniquely their own.

As the construction of each individual block had the advantage of economy in both materials and space, it had much to recommend it to the early settlers, for whom both were in short supply. Only when enough blocks were finished to make the quilt top was more room needed to assemble, quilt and finish the piece. These later stages of the quilt were often done quickly as a cooperative effort at a quilting bee.

Both pieced patchwork and appliqué can be made in block format and often the two techniques are combined in designs such as "Carolina Lily" or the numerous basket blocks. Block patterns were often identified by names which referred to local and national events, stories from the Bible or characters from public life, for example "Flying Geese," "Sherman's March," "Jacob's Ladder" and "Martha Washington's Star." To some

extent block names were dependent on locale; the same block is known variously as "Duck's Foot in the Mud," "Hand of Friendship" and "Bear's Paw."

Block patterns

Block patterns fall into different categories. The one-patch uses just one single shape, but within this limitation order can be imposed by organizing the colors and values to create designs. A good example is the "Thousand Pyramids" block, which uses equilateral triangles. By the simple device of placing all the dark triangles pointing upward and all the light ones downward, the dark triangles combine to give the illusion in the name.

Sets of blocks containing a combination of shapes take their name from the grid which can be imposed over the design. Four-patch and nine-patch are the most numerous but there are also many irregular blocks. By breaking down the block into its basic grid you can determine the order of construction. Start with the smallest pieces and wherever possible work in straight lines.

Secondary patterns

It is only when you start placing blocks edge to edge that the secondary designs start to appear. The shapes merge together to form a complex overall design, and frequently make it difficult to identify the individual block. Once this concept is understood, it can be exploited to dynamic effect by the careful choice of colors, textures and values in the fabrics (see page 148).

If, rather than create these secondary designs, you want to preserve the identity of individual block patterns, they can be separated by sashing, strips of fabric often in plain colors which divide the blocks and give a lattice effect. This technique is often used with album quilts, those in which each block is different. To set such blocks edge to edge would create a confused jumble of different shapes.

By turning the block into a diamond shape, or setting it "on point," a totally different effect can be achieved. In this case the edges of the quilt must be filled with triangles to finish the square or rectangular shape.

Combining and alternating two blocks can create even more complex secondary designs, and alternate plain and patchwork blocks will provide plain areas for elaborate quilting patterns.

From simple beginnings using folded paper as the basis for designs, infinite possibilities have been developed and remain to be explored.

Three types of block patterns, used in quilts made by Katharine Guerrier. From far left to right: *Jacob's Ladder*, *Thousand Pyramids* and a secondary pattern, formed by the careful juxtaposition of individual blocks.

BLOCK CONSTRUCTION

Although sewing machines are now frequently considered a normal part of household equipment, many people still prefer to sew patchwork by hand. Quilters give various reasons: the fact that it makes a project more portable, with the advantage of being able to sit with the family while working on a quilt, or the slower pace of construction which gives time for making decisions about what color or where to put the next piece of fabric, or even for the sheer nostalgic value that somehow puts them in spiritual contact with quiltmakers from a previous era. If you want fast results, however, a machine-sewn quilt is a more realistic proposition. Many contemporary quilters combine the two by machine-piecing and hand-quilting; no machine can emulate the unique properties of beautiful hand-quilting.

Hand-sewing

If hand-sewing, you will need to mark the stitching line by drawing round the templates on the wrong side of the fabric. Add in the seam allowance before you cut out the patches. Begin and end stitching at each seam line (not the edge of the fabric), starting with a small knot or backstitch and ending firmly with a backstitch. Press seams to one side – where possible, the darker side.

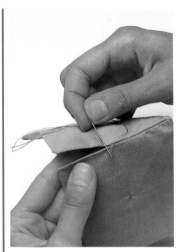

Machine-sewing

When sewing patches together by machine, it is not necessary to mark a stitching line. Just place the patches right sides together, pin, then guide the raw edges of the fabric against the presser foot of the machine. The foot on most sewing machines will automatically give ¼ inch seam allowance. If yours does not, mark the plate on your machine with a narrow strip of masking tape parallel to the seam line ¼ inch from the needle. Alternatively, check out whether the "Little Foot" developed especially for patchwork will fit your machine. your machine. This will measure the seam allowance for you at exactly ¼ inch from the edge.

Basic piecing techniques

1 Chain-piecing is a quick way of piecing together a quantity of patches.

Place the patches right sides together and sew with a running stitch by hand or machine.

2 Cut chain-pieced patches apart and press seams. Machine-sewn seams are strong enough to be pressed open, or they can be pressed to one side.

Piecing order

It is important to insure that all the patches are organized in the correct order before **any** stitching takes place.

1 When all the patches are cut out, spread them out on a flat surface in the correct position. Make up the squares.

Nancy Breland,
Mosaic (detail)
Accurate piecing of the blocks in the quilt contribute to the complex secondary designs.

2 Set the squares together in rows.

3 Join the rows to form one block.

Setting in
Stitch straight lines where possible. Some blocks, however, need to have pieces "set in" to a right-angled corner.

1 Stitch the first seam up to the ¼-inch seam allowance to create the right angle.

2 Stitch the piece to be set in along one edge, then pivot through the right angle and stitch along the other edge.

3 Press the seam away from the set-in patch.

4 The finished unit seen from the front.

Piecing angled shapes
When joining shapes that have angles other than 90 degrees – diamonds and triangles – align the stitching lines, *not* the cut edges. This makes a straight edge when the patches are opened.

Matching points
Many blocks have a point at which four or more different fabrics meet.

1 To match these points accurately, push a pin through at the exact spot where the points are to be matched, at a right angle to the stitching line. Stitch up to the pin.

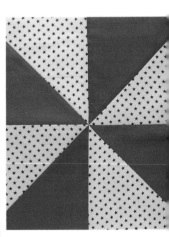

2 Remove carefully and then stitch over the point.

Piecing curved seams

If the block has curved seams, as in the "Drunkard's Path" pattern, concave and convex edges must be joined.

1 Cut pieces and mark the center points. Clip into the concave curve *within* the ¼-inch seam allowance (no more than ⅛ inch).

2 Pin these center points and the ends together, then ease the curves to fit, putting in several pins to hold them.

3 Sew along the stitching line by hand or machine with the concave curved piece on top and keeping the raw edges together as you sew.

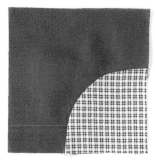

4 Press seams toward the patch with the convex curve.

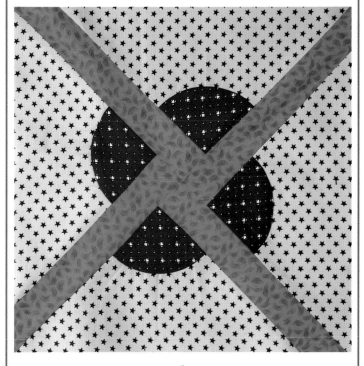

Josephine Knot

This complex-looking design is made from four sections. These are combined in diagonals to form the final design.

FOUR-PATCH BLOCKS

The most effective solution to a design problem is often the simplest, and the four-patch block has the virtue of simplicity built into its structure. The basic block is just what its name suggests; four equal-sized squares of fabric stitched together. To make the block more complex, these squares can be subdivided within the grid. The "Pinwheel" and "Broken Dishes" blocks have the squares divided into half-square triangles. The composition of the four-patch block for the "Pinwheel" pattern is shown in detail on these two pages. By contrast, the "Big Dipper" and "Hovering Hawks" blocks use quarter-squares. A darker rectangle cuts diagonally across each of the four equal squares in "Devil's Puzzle."

"Star" blocks are always popular and two which fall into the four-patch family are "Ribbon Star" and "Pierced Star." There are dozens of other four-patch blocks, some of which become subdivided into 4 × 4 or even 8 × 8 equal divisions, but as long as it is possible to impose an equal 2 × 2 grid over a design, it is four-patch.

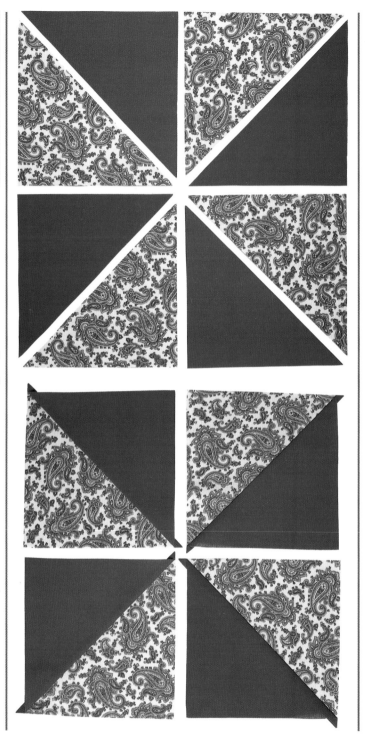

Constructing a four-patch block

1 Place patches in the required position on a flat surface.

2 Join the triangles first to make four squares. Seams can be pressed open or to one side.

3 Next, join the squares to make two rectangles, matching the points.

4 Finally, join the two rectangles to make the square, matching the points of the center of the block.

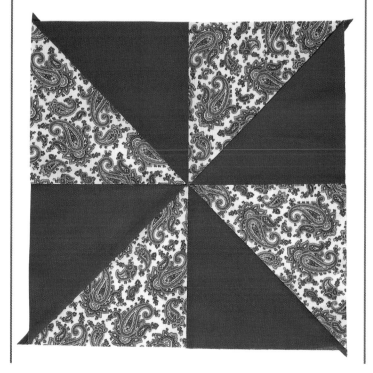

Four-patch blocks
"Big Dipper" The contrast between light and dark creates the counterchange in the design.

"Broken Dishes" Dark, medium and light values are used in this simple block.

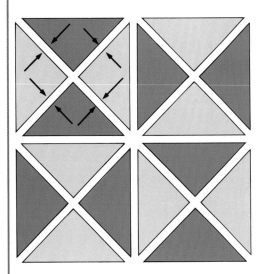

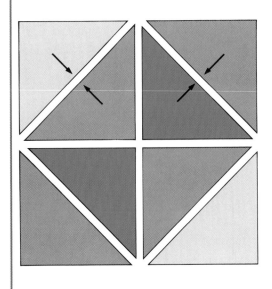

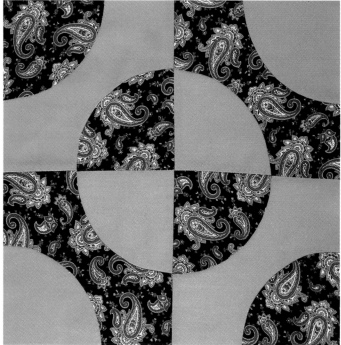

"Devil's Puzzle" Placed edge to edge, the blocks in this design will create a strong secondary design with diagonal emphasis.

"Robbing Peter to Pay Paul"
A four-patch block which makes use of curved seams.

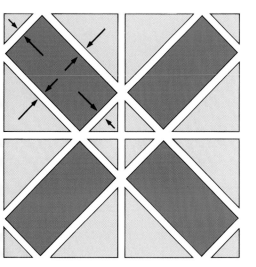

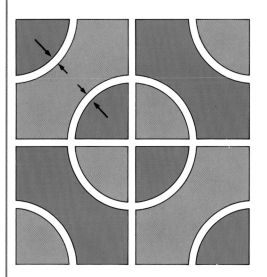

NINE-PATCH BLOCKS

As its name suggests, the nine-patch block is divided into a 3 × 3 grid. Examples of this type that are simple to piece include "Friendship Star," "Shoofly" and "Ohio Star." The composition of the nine-patch block for the "Shoofly" pattern is shown in detail on these two pages. A vast variety of different designs can be created by dividing the grid in more complex ways, some presenting more of a challenge than others. "Card Trick," for example, uses the juxtaposition of different colors to create a three-dimensional effect. Secondary designs are also important in many nine-block quilts, as in the intriguingly titled "Contrary Wife." Whatever your choice, plan the design with consideration of the tonal values of the fabrics to be used. Placing the emphasis on another part of a block can make it look completely different. Try shading the same block design in different tonal combinations. The results are often surprising.

Some of the most interesting nine patch blocks are featured on the following pages.

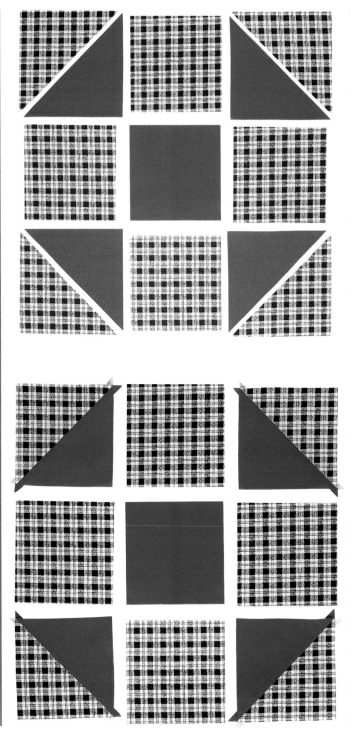

Constructing a nine-patch block

1 Arrange the patches in the required order on a flat surface.

2 Join the triangles to form squares. Press seams open or to the darker side.

3 Stitch the squares into three rows as shown.

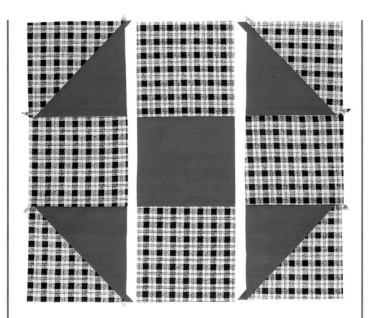

4 Stitch the three rows together to make up the block.

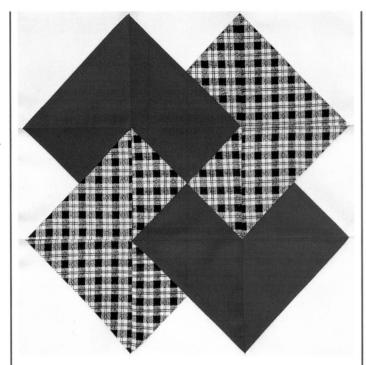

Nine-patch blocks
"Card Trick" This block has an intriguing three-dimensional effect created by placement of dark, medium and light fabrics.

"Palm Leaf" One of a number of "leaf" blocks.

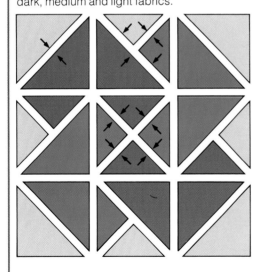

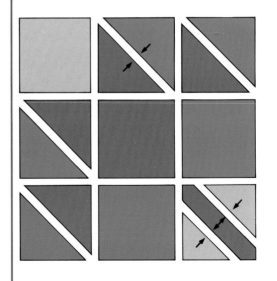

"Contrary Wife" Strong
secondary designs emerge
when blocks are placed edge
to edge.

**"Fifty-four Forty or
Fight"** This interesting title
refers to the dispute between
the United States and British

Canada over the division of the
Pacific Northwest in 1846.

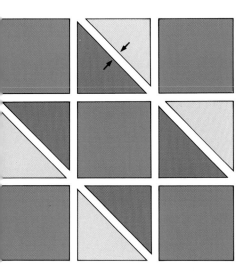

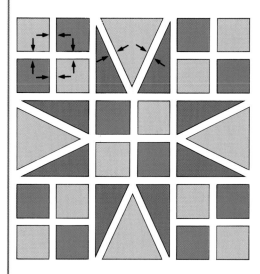

IRREGULAR BLOCKS

The whole area of block classification can be confusing when you start to study patchwork; even within the simpler categories of four- and nine-patch blocks, there is some overlap. For this reason the blocks which cannot easily be fitted into either of these sets are here termed as "irregular" blocks. By analyzing the shapes within the block, and determining the grid which fits over the block – whether it be equal units of 5×5, 7×7 or any other combination, it becomes clear how the pieces will fit together, and the block can be constructed. The same rules apply: smaller shapes combine to make larger ones, and sew in straight lines wherever this is possible.

"Cake Stand" This is a popular "picture" block because the design is simple and good for using up scraps.

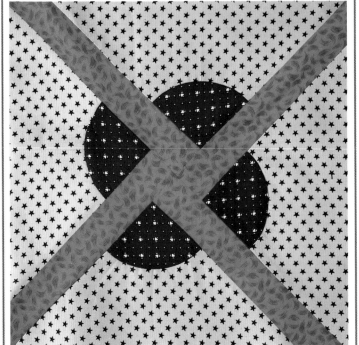

"Josephine Knot" This block is split diagonally with each quarter-section made up of only three pieces.

"Old Maid's Ramble"
Fragmented triangles in opposing values create the counterchange effect.

"Assymetrical blocks" These can be designed within the framework of any grid.

"LOG CABIN"

Popular among the traditional designs, "Log Cabin" quilts are often seen to have a significance beyond their qualities of graphic design, representing home in the hostile conditions that faced the pioneers.

Although "Log Cabin" quilts were known to have been made in Europe, the design is largely associated with the early settlers in the United States, and it has maintained its popularity up to the present day. The construction of the "Log Cabin" block is straightforward; strips of fabric rotate around a center square, traditionally red to represent the fire or hearth. The block is split diagonally into light and dark fabrics to create the illusion of shadows and flickering firelight within the cabin. There are variations to this basic pattern, but they all rely on the visual play of light and dark tonal values. Although a single block looks simple, the versatility of the design can only be realized when the blocks are placed together in multiples, and their secondary designs become apparent. Dozens of different variations are possible, all with great visual impact and all of which exploit the contrast between the dark and light

fabrics with graphic simplicity. There are many named designs such as "Barn Raising", "Courthouse Steps" and "Sunshine and Shadow" plus numerous others that can all be made by using combinations of the basic block.

Traditionally, the block is stitched onto a square of foundation fabric – this stabilizes the fabrics and encloses the seams on the back. Decide on the finished size of your block; 12 to 15 inches would be suitable for a quilt, a panel of four blocks 8 to 9 inches square would make a cushion front. Plan the design on graph paper to determine measurements. Three factors will affect the finished size of the block: the dimensions of the center square, the width of the strips, and how many rounds of strips are used.

1 Cut a square of foundation fabric – white sheeting or calico – about 1½ inches larger than the desired finished size of the block. Press diagonal creases with a steam iron, then place the center square, right side up, on the foundation square with the corners on the diagonal creases.

2 This ensures that the block center is positioned in the middle of the foundation square.

Sort out the fabrics into light and dark colors. All pieces – centers and strips – can be cut with the rotary-cutting set. Add seam allowances as you cut. For a 2-inch finished center square cut 2½ × 2½ inches. For 1-inch finished strips, cut strips 1½ inches wide.

Select a different colored fabric from the lighter pile. Cut a strip the desired width and the length of one side of the center square. Place this right side down on the center square, raw edges together. Pin and stitch through the three layers taking a ¼-inch seam allowance.

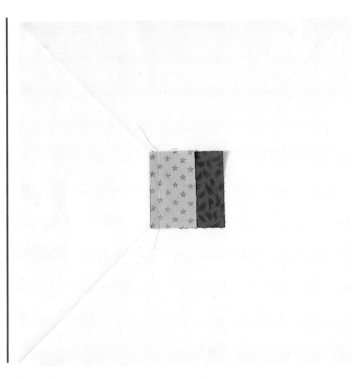

Turn the strip over to reveal the right side of the fabric, and then press flat against the foundation.

5 Turn the foundation square through 90 degrees anticlockwise, and place the second strip – using the same fabric – right side down against the center and short edge of the first strip. Align the raw edges, then stitch down through all layers as before. Fold this strip back and press.

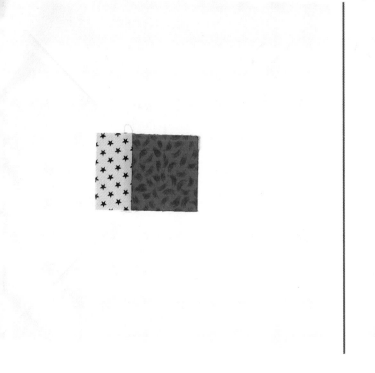

6 Turn the foundation through another 90 degrees counterclockwise, then select a fabric from a contrasting, darker pile. Cut a strip, and add this to the block in the same way. Turn and press flat against the foundation.

7 The fourth strip completes the first round. This will establish which is to be the dark side of the block and which the light side.

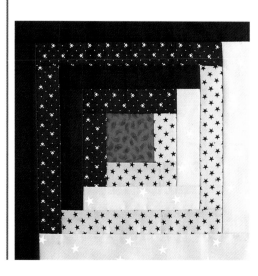

8 Continue to add strips, maintaining the correct light/dark sequence until the block is complete. (The sequence for arranging the strips is shown in the numbered diagram, right). Trim away the foundation to the edges of the last round of strips, leaving ¼-inch seam allowance all around for joining the blocks together. Arrange the blocks in the design required, and place them right sides together, then stitch through all layers taking ¼-inch seam allowance.

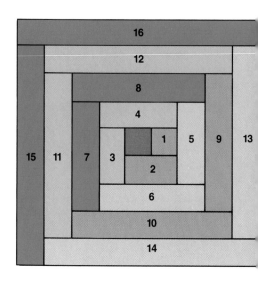

"Courthouse Steps"

In this variation strips are sewn on opposite sides of the center square in an alternate dark/light sequence, so a quite different effect is achieved. This pattern is sometimes also known as "Chinese Lanterns."

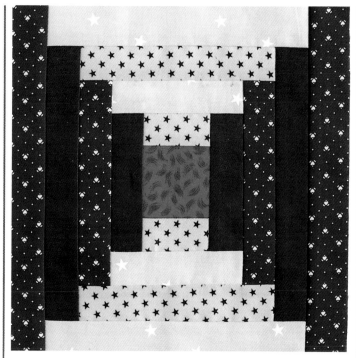

"Sunshine and Shadow"

The width of the strips can be varied. In this version the lighter colored strips are wider than the dark ones, giving the effect of curved lines. The "Sunshine and Shadow" design can also be done with strips of the same width.

"Barn Raising"

An arrangement of the blocks which results in concentric diamonds of alternating dark and light colored fabrics.

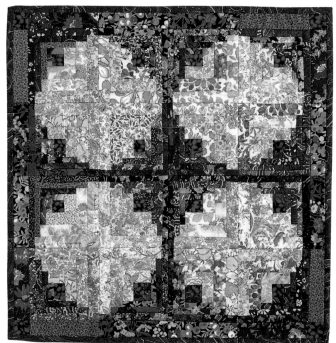

ROTARY-CUTTING

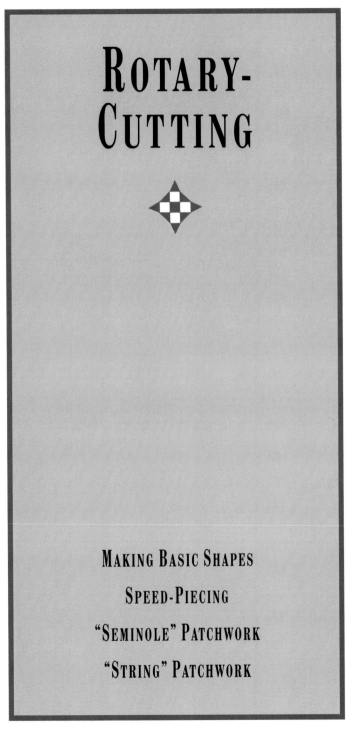

MAKING BASIC SHAPES

SPEED-PIECING

"SEMINOLE" PATCHWORK

"STRING" PATCHWORK

The pressures of modern living have brought demands to speed up the process of quilt-making. The introduction of rotary-cutting has made this very easy by eliminating much of the time spent in cutting the patches. Templates are not used for rotary-cutting – except for curved seams – and seam allowances are included in the overall dimensions of the pieces when they are cut.

The rotary-cutting set

Although there are many tools and rulers available, everything can be done with just a few tools. The four essentials are a rotary cutter, a board, a square and a ruler. The rotary cutter is a circular blade set in a handle with a safety lock. It is important to get into the habit of using this lock each time that you put the cutter down. The board is made from a score-resistant material which will not blunt the blade and is made in a variety of sizes. The ruler is made of thick clear plastic with a straight, non-bevelled edge, and also is available in a variety of sizes.

A good basic set would include a large rotary cutter, a board 24 × 18 inches, and a ruler 6 × 24 inches. In addition you need a square; a 6 inch bias square is the most useful.

With this equipment you will be able to cut and subcut strips into many geometrical shapes. However, to be successful, you need to use the equipment accurately and safely. The ruler and the board are marked with a grid, but you are advised to use the grid on the ruler and not that on the board. The ruler is laser-printed, but the board is printed with the use of rollers and can on some occasions be inaccurate. To save confusion, use the board plain-side up.

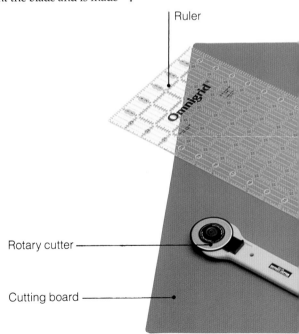

Ruler

Rotary cutter

Cutting board

Setting up and squaring the fabric

1 Place the washed and ironed fabric on the board with the fold towards you and the selvedges away from you. Any surplus fabric should lie away to the side of your cutting hand. Place the square on the folded edge of the fabric close to the edge that you will cut. Place the ruler next to the square with one of the horizontal lines on the edge of the fabric. The edge of the ruler should butt up to the square. Hold the ruler down firmly, and slide the square away.

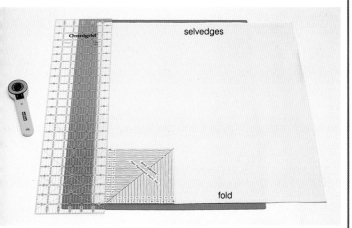

selvedges

fold

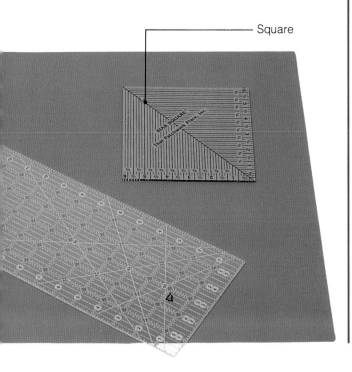

Square

2 Holding the ruler steady, open the cutter, and place the blade next to the ruler. Start cutting, pushing the cutter firmly away from you with an even pressure as you do so. When the cutter comes level with your hand, stop cutting, but maintain the pressure.

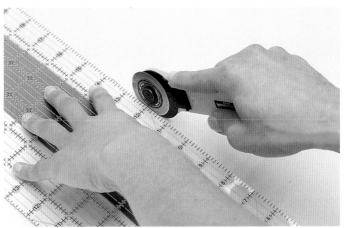

3 Move your hand up the ruler to a new position, and then cut again to a point level with your hand. Keep repeating until you reach the selvedges.

Remember to move only one hand at a time, either the one cutting or the one holding the ruler. This initial squaring-up cut is the only time that you cut through only the two thicknesses of fabric.

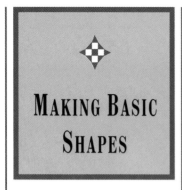

MAKING BASIC SHAPES

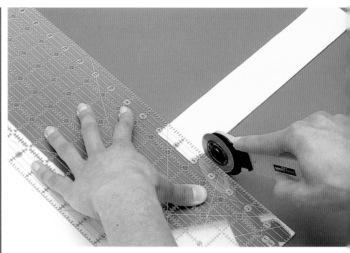

Cutting strips

1 Fold the fabric over in half again so that the folded edge is positioned on top of the selvedges and all the cut edges match.

2 To cut a strip, place a horizontal line on the fold of the fabric and the line indicating your desired width along the cut edges. Keeping a horizontal line on the fold at all times will prevent you from cutting strips with "V"-shapes at the folds. When the ruler is in the correct position, hold the ruler in place with your hand – firmly splayed in the middle of your ruler – and cut with the blade against the ruler. Starting ahead of the fold, cut with an even pressure across the fabric. If you are going to subcut these strips, leave them folded.

3 Remember when cutting strips to add a seam allowance of ¼ inch to each side of the strip before you cut.

Cutting squares

1 Take a cut strip and place it across the board with the double fold to the right if you are right-handed, and to the left, if you are left-handed.

Place a horizontal line of the ruler on the lower edge of the strip, and cut a small strip from the selvedge edge to straighten the end of the strip.

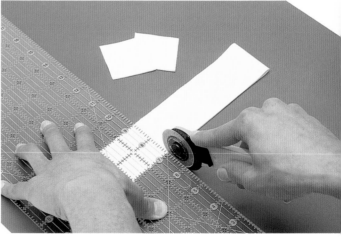

2 Place a horizontal line on the edge of the strip and the vertical line of the square measurement along the straightened end of the strip, and cut the square. You will have four in a stack. Continue cutting the squares until you have the required number. If necessary, you may need to straighten the vertical edge again occasionally.

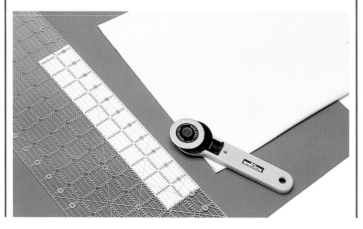

Subcutting into rectangles

1 Position the ready-cut strip on the board and straighten the end, as you did for a square. Then, with a horizontal line on the lower edge and the vertical measurement on the straightened edge, cut a rectangle from the strip.

2 If the length of the rectangle is longer than the width of the ruler, simply turn the ruler through 90 degrees and use the other way round.

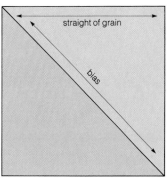

straight of grain

bias

Subcutting into half-square triangles

1 A half-square triangle is illustrated above. It is used whenever the shorter edges of the triangle are parallel to the edge of the block or quilt.

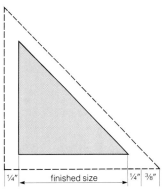

¼" finished size ¼" ⅜"

2 To cut a half-square triangle, a square is cut and then cut again diagonally. So that sufficient fabric is allowed for seam allowances all around, it is important to consider the triangle drawn on graph paper. Add ¼ inch all around, and then measure the short side. It will be ⅞ inch longer than the finished size of the triangle. *Rule for half-square triangles:* finished size plus ⅞ inch.

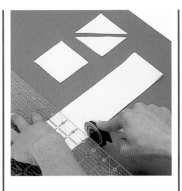

3 Cut a strip the width of the finished size of the triangle plus ⅞ inch, and cut a square the same width.

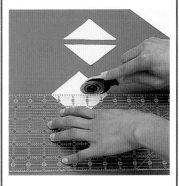

4 Place the ruler across the diagonal of the square, and cut the stack of squares into two stacks of triangles. Repeat for more triangles.

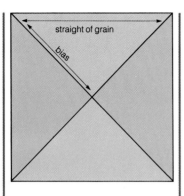

straight of grain

bias

Subcutting into quarter-square triangles

1 A quarter-square triangle is illustrated above. It is used whenever the longer edge of the triangle is parallel to the edge of the block or quilt.

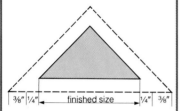

3⁄8" 1⁄4" finished size 1⁄4" 3⁄8"

2 To make a quarter-square triangle, a square is cut and then cut again on both diagonals. To insure that sufficient fabric is allowed, it is worth looking at the triangle drawn on graph paper. Add 1⁄4 inch all around, and then measure the long side. It will be 1 1⁄4 inches longer than the finished size of the triangle.
Rule for quarter-square triangles: finished size plus 1 1⁄4 inches.

3 Cut a strip the width of the finished size of the triangle plus 1 1⁄4 inches and then cut a square the same width.

4 Place the ruler across the diagonal and cut. *Do not* move the pieces.

5 Place the ruler across the other diagonal and cut. You will now have four stacks of quarter-square triangles. Repeat the process for more triangles.

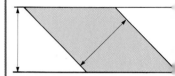

Subcutting into diamonds

1 Diamonds either have 45-degree or 60-degree angles. The distance between the parallel sides are always equal. The strips that you cut are the same as the distance between the parallel sides plus the seam allowances.

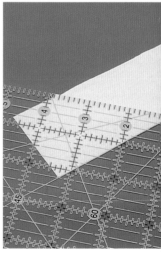

2 When the strip is cut, you need to set up the angle of 45 degrees at one end by pivoting the ruler till the 45-degree line lies along the bottom edge of the strip.

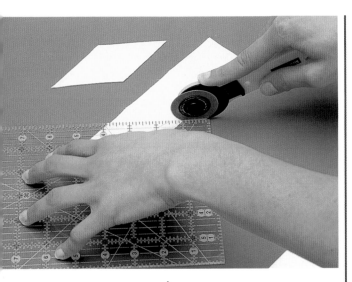

3 To cut diamonds, keep the 45-degree line on the bottom edge of the strip, and slide the ruler across till the angled edge is on the line of the measurement of the strip. Repeat the process as necessary for more diamonds.

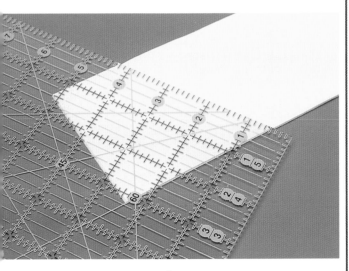

4 To cut 60-degree diamonds, you should follow the same process. However, this time use the 60-degree line along the bottom edge of the strip.

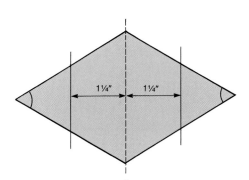

Subcutting a 60-degree diamond into a hexagon

1 First cut the diamonds. Let us assume the measurement used is 2½ inches.

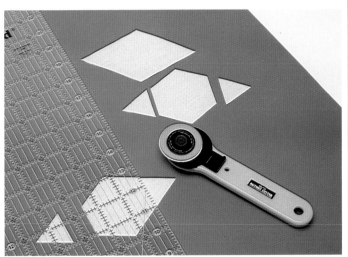

2 To change the diamond into a hexagon, cut the long points off. Measure half the original measurement (i.e. 1¼ inches) from the short diagonal and cut. Turn the diamond round, and make the opposite cut the same way.

Subcutting strips into trapezoids

1 It can be seen from the diagram that the rule for a trapezoid with one point is the same as that for a half-square triangle. Add ⅞ inch to the finished size of the base.

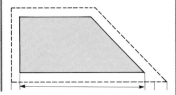

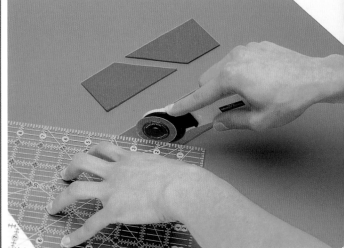

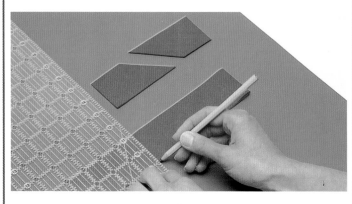

2 Using a strip that is the width of the trapezoid plus the seam allowances, straighten the left edge.

3 From the left edge, measure the base measurement plus ⅞ inch. Mark a dot on the bottom edge of the strip.

4 Placing the 45-degree line on the bottom edge of the strip and the edge of the ruler on the dot, cut at a 45-degree angle.

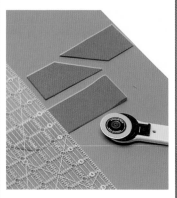

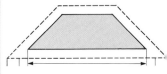

5 For the next cut, measure the length of the trapezoid plus ⅞ inch along the top edge of the strip, and cut straight. You are then ready to repeat the process for more trapezoids.

6 From the diagram, you can see that the rule for a trapezoid with two points is the same as that for a quarter-square triangle. Add 1¼ inches to the finished length of the base.

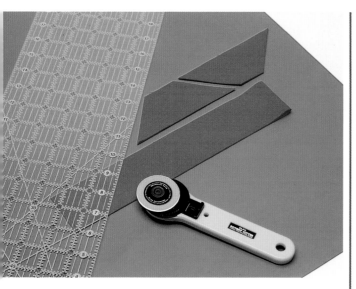

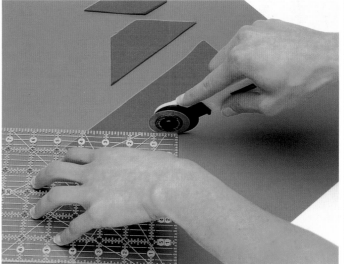

7 Using a strip the width of the trapezoid plus seam allowances with the 45-degree line on the bottom edge of the strip, cut the left-hand end at a 45-degree angle.

9 With the 45-degree line on the bottom edge of the strip and the edge of the ruler on the dot, cut at a 45-degree angle in the opposite direction to the first cut.

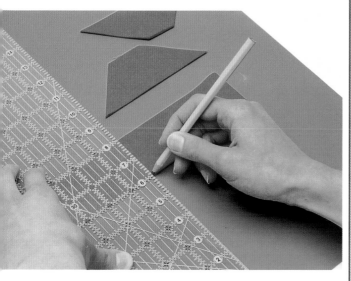

8 Measure along the bottom edge the length of the trapezoid plus 1¼ inches and mark with a dot.

10 The point is established. Now measure the length of the base plus 1¼ inches along the top edge of the strip. Mark with a dot.

11 Keeping the 45-degree line along the top edge and the edge of the ruler on the dot, cut at a 45-degree angle. Repeat the process for more trapezoids.

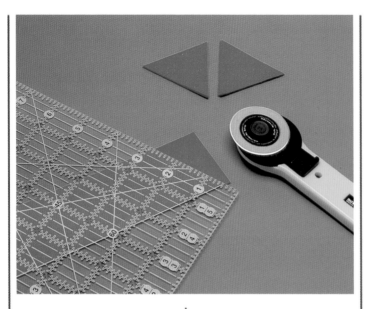

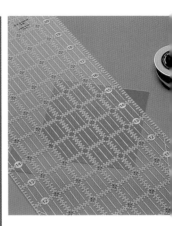

Subcutting strips into 60-degree triangles

1 Using strips the width of the height of the triangle plus seam allowances, place the 60- degree line along the bottom edge of the strip. Cut out the strip at a 60-degree angle on the right-hand edge.

Subcutting squares into octagons

1 Using cut squares, mark lines diagonally across the square.

2 Measuring from the center, cut the corner of the square off at a distance half the width of the original square.

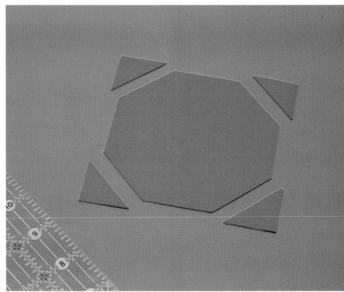

2 Pivot the ruler on the 60-degree line so that the other 60-degree line is now on the bottom edge of the strip and the edge of the ruler is on the top edge at the cut. Cut at a 60- degree angle.

3 Pivot the ruler again and you are ready to make the third cut. Repeat the process to produce more triangles.

3 Repeat for the other corners.

SPEED-PIECING

Once you have mastered the rotary cutter, there are many quilt patterns that can be cut and pieced quickly. For example, "Log Cabin" blocks can be made more efficiently if you can cut straight strips. Some quilt designs require you to sew the strips together before you cut. The simplest of these is a "Rail Fence," but there are many others such as "Simple Four-Patch," "Nine Patch," "Irish Chain" and "Trip Around The World."

Most patchwork blocks break down into simple shapes that can be cut with the rotary cutter. If a quilt is made of lots of repeated blocks, it is best to do the cutting for all the blocks at once rather than one at a time. Also when a design calls for many half-square triangles, these can be created by using a "Grid Method" to save time. However, if you are only making one block, you can use the method set out for the "Friendship Star."

Nine-patch block

The measurements given here are for a 6-inch finished block. To change the size of the block, determine the desired finished size of the patch and add ½ inch to the width of the strips as you cut them. Use the same measurement as the width of the strips to cut the cross sections, e.g., for a 9½-inch block the patch measures 3 inches, so cut strips and sections of 3½ inches.

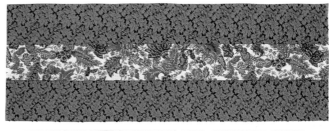

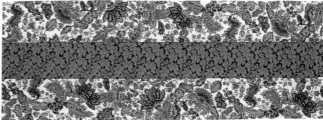

1 Cut three dark and three light strips – 2½ inches wide across the width of the fabric. Seam them together (taking a ¼-in seam allowance) in two sets of three: dark/light/dark and light/dark/light.

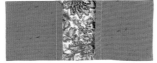

2 Press seams to one side – toward the center strip on one set and away from the center strip on the other. Place the two sets right sides together, matching the seams. Straighten one short end, then cut into 2½-inch strips across the seams.

3 Arrange the desired nine-patch and stitch. The seams will match as they lock together.

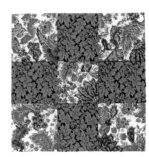

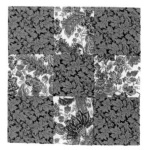

4 The final seams can be pressed open or to one side as preferred.

"Pinwheel" and "Broken Dishes"

The measurements given here are for a 6-inch finished block. To change the size of the block, add ⅞ inch to the size of the finished unit when cutting the squares, e.g., for a 8-inch block the unit would be 4 inches, so cut squares 4⅞ inches.

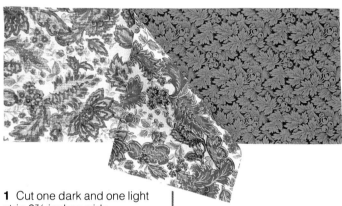

1 Cut one dark and one light strip 3⅞ inches wide the width of the fabric. Place these, right sides together, straighten one short side and cut into four squares 3⅞ inches.

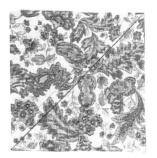

2 Mark one diagonal line on the wrong side of one of the fabric squares.

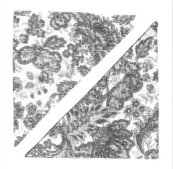

3 Taking a ¼-inch seam allowance, sew on either side of the line and cut on the line.

4 Press seams and arrange the resulting units in the desired block pattern.

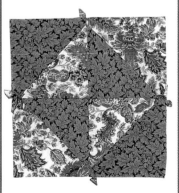

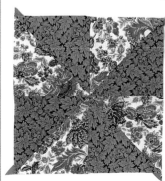

"Pinwheel"

"Broken Dishes"

"Letter X"

The measurements given here are for a 6-inch finished block. To change the size of the block, add 1¼-inch to the finished size of the unit.

Many blocks are made from units of squares, rectangles, half-square triangles, and quarter-square triangles and they can all be constructed using quick piecing methods.

3 One set of squares will make two units. Cut the plain squares 2½ × 2½ inches.

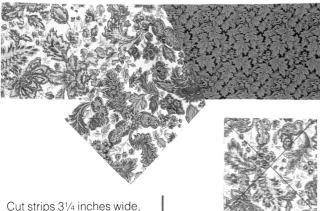

Cut strips 3¼ inches wide, from dark and light fabric. Place these strips, right sides together, straighten one short edge and cut into squares. Mark two diagonal lines on the wrong side of one of the fabrics.

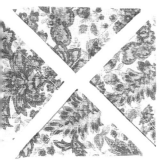
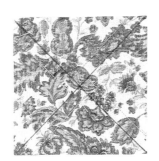

Stitch to the center on the left-hand side of the lines, then cut along the drawn lines.

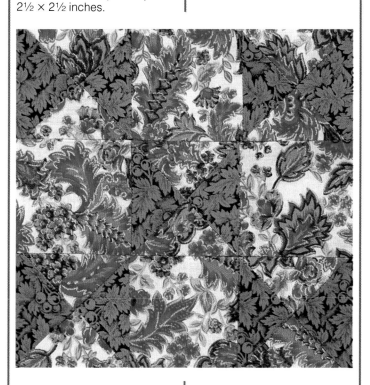

4 Arrange the units as shown for the "Letter X block."

"Ohio Star" block

This block also uses square and quarter-square triangle units. It is a nine-patch block. For a 12-inch block, the size of the finished unit is 4 inches.

Cut the squares 4½ × 4½ inches, four light and one dark colored. For the triangle units cut two dark colored squares 5¼ × 5¼ inches and two light colored squares 5¼ × 5¼ inches. The squares are 1¼ inch larger than the size of the finished unit.

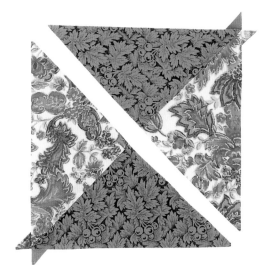

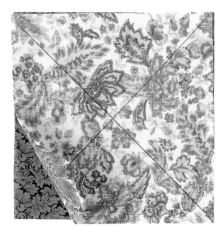

1 Place these squares right sides together and steam-press. Draw two diagonal lines across the square (on the wrong side of the fabric), dividing it into quarters, and sew ¼ inch to the left of each line in each quarter, from the edge of the fabric to the point at which the lines cross.

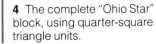

3 Two of the resulting triangles, one each of equally sized dark and light triangles, can be seamed together to make one unit made of four half-square triangles.

4 The complete "Ohio Star" block, using quarter-square triangle units.

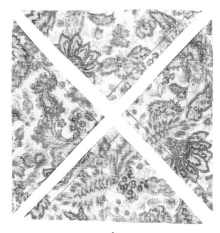

2 Cut along the drawn diagonal lines, open out the resulting triangles and press flat.

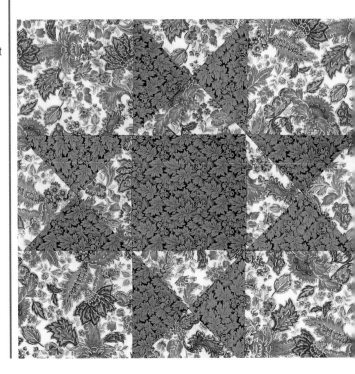

"Friendship Star" block

This block will require four light squares 4½ × 4½ inches, one dark square 4½ × 4½ inches. For the triangle units, two light squares 4⅞ × 4⅞ inches. For squares or rectangles, add ¼ inch all around to the desired finished size of the shape. For half-square triangles, add ⅞ inch to the size of the square. For this block, you will need two squares each of the dark and light fabric 4⅞ × 4⅞ inches.

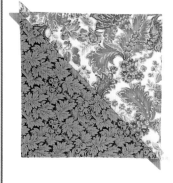

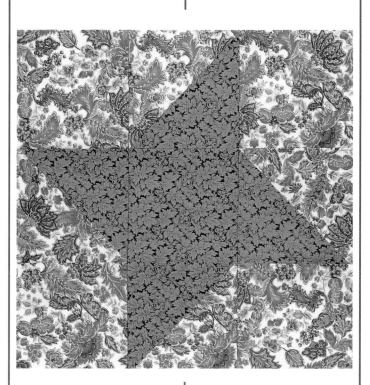

4 This will make two half-square triangle units 4½ × 4½ inches.

Place one dark and one light-colored square right sides together, and steam-press. Draw one diagonal line across the squares.

3 Cut along the drawn line.

Stitch on both sides of the line, taking ¼-inch seam allowance.

5 Arrange the units as illustrated with the squares to complete the block.

"Flying Geese"

If a different-size unit is required, just cut the small squares into half the size of the large one and add ¼ inch.

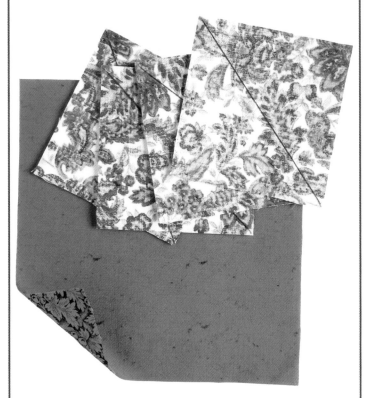

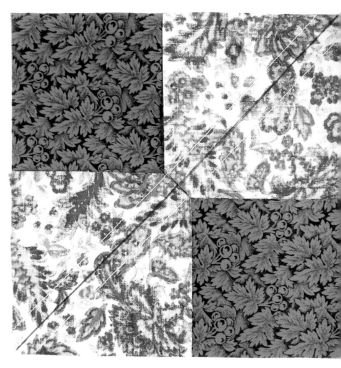

1 Cut one square of "goose" fabric 6 × 6 inches and four squares of background fabric 3¼ × 3¼ inches. Mark one diagonal line on each of the background squares on the wrong side of the fabric.

2 Lay the larger square flat, right-side up, and place one small square in the corner, right side down. Snip off the corner where it crosses the center of the larger square. Pin another square in the opposite corner, trim the corner off this one also. Sew from corner to corner ¼ inch on either side of the diagonal line.

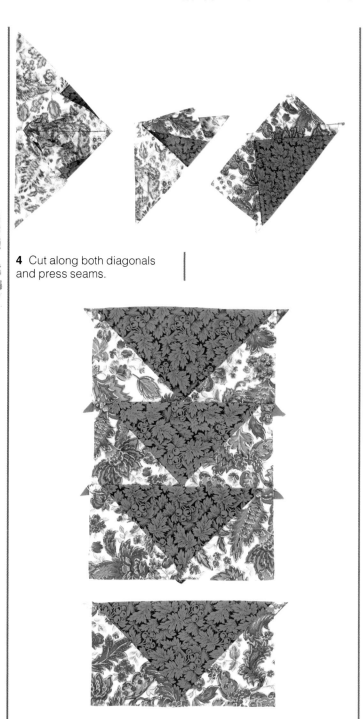

4 Cut along both diagonals and press seams.

3 Pin the sides of the smaller squares away from the center, place the other two smaller squares in the remaining corners and trim off the center corners as before. Sew on either side of the marked diagonal line as before.

5 This unit will make four "flying geese."

A "Log Cabin" block

It is possible to piece "Log Cabin" blocks together without the foundation square. Just cut the center squares and strips as for the foundation method and, starting with the center and strip A, place, right sides together and stitch, taking the usual ¼-inch seam allowance. Press the strip away from the center, then continue adding the strips in the correct light and dark sequence. If several identical blocks are required, use this quick piecing method.

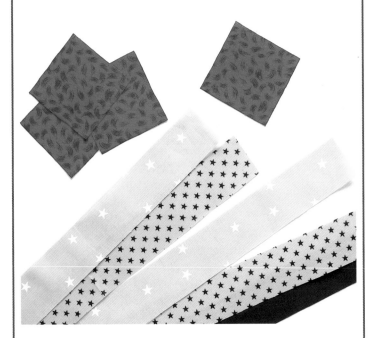

1 Cut the required number of strips and squares from your chosen fabric.

2 Sew all the center squares to strip A as indicated, leaving a small gap between each one.

3 Trim the strips to size and press each.

Front

Front

Join these units to strip B in the same way as shown.

Front

Continue, keeping light and dark colored fabrics in the correct sequence.

Front

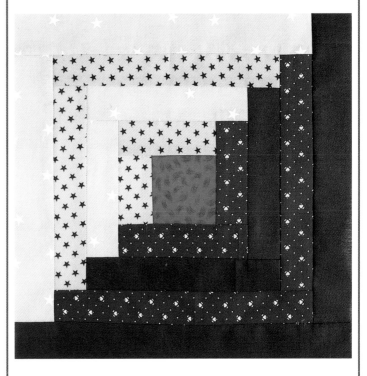

The complete "Log Cabin" block uses contrasting areas of light and dark color to make dramatic impact.

"SEMINOLE" PATCHWORK

The Seminole Indians of Florida devised this ingenious form of patchwork in the late 19th century, when trading with white settlers made hand-cranked sewing machines available. Long strips of fabric are first stitched together, then cut and reassembled into dozens of different designs. Plain, bright colors are the most effective, providing contrast between the characteristic small geometric shapes. The resulting strips of patchwork were used to decorate clothing, household textiles or even dolls.

Measurements can be scaled up or down as long as the ratio remains the same. Approximately one-third of the cut width of the strips is lost when the finished design is pieced. Designs can be reversed, offset or angled to give different effects.

Basically, strips are cut across the full width of the fabric. If using scissors, measure and mark the line to cut on for accuracy. The rotary-cutting set is an ideal way of cutting the strips quickly and accurately. When stitching the strips together, use a shorter than normal stitch on your sewing machine to prevent the seam from coming undone when the seamed strips are cut into sections. Take ¼-inch seam allowance. Avoid pleats on the front by gently pressing strips apart with your fingers as you iron the seam allowance to one side.

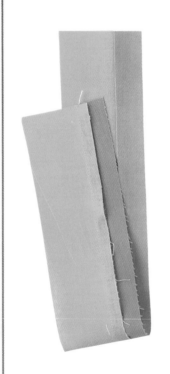

Simple reversed designs using two colors

1 Cut two strips in contrasting colors, one 1-inch wide and the other 1¾-inches wide. Sew the two strips right sides together, taking ¼-inch seam allowance.

2 Press the seam to one side on the back, then press the right side. Cut into 1-inch sections across the strips.

3 Reverse alternate sections as shown.

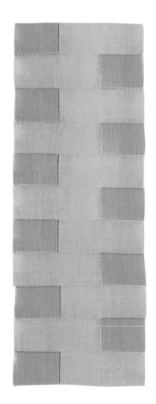

4 Stitch the sections together in this sequence.

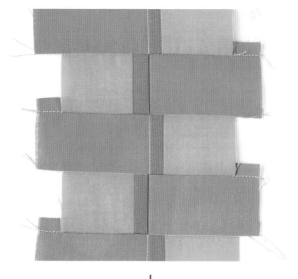

3 Reverse alternate sections and stitch back together, aligning the corners of the narrow strip as above.

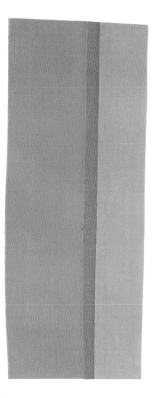

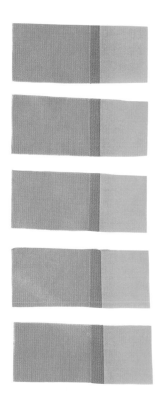

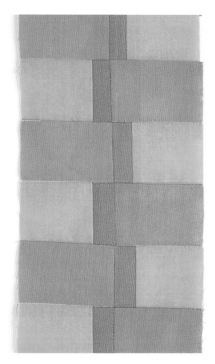

Reversed design using three colors

1 Cut three strips in the following widths: 1½-inches, ¾-inch and 2¼-inches and seam together.

2 Cut across the strips in sections 1½-inches wide.

4 Trim away the excess fabric at the sides, as shown.

Offset design using two colors

Work across the width of the fabric so you have 44-inch lengths. One strip should be dark and one light.

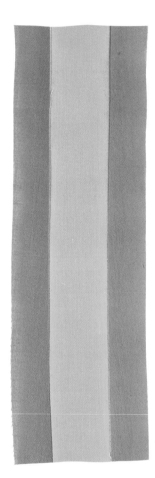

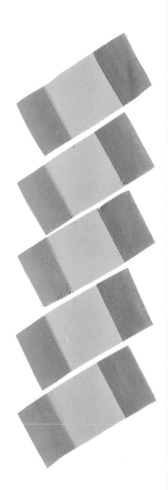

1 In the dark fabric cut two strips 1-inch wide. In the light fabric cut one strip 1¾-inch wide. Taking ¼-inch seam allowance, stitch the strips together as shown in the picture. Press the seams to one side.

2 Cut across the strips in 1¼-inch pieces. Mark a dot at the top of the light strip, positioned ½-inch in from the left-hand seam. Place the cut pieces, right sides together, with the left-hand seam against the dot. This will offset each piece by ½-inch.

3 Continue to stitch the pieces together until enough length is created. Be careful to maintain accuracy when matching the dot to the seam.

4 Trim away the points at the sides, remembering to leave ¼-inch seam allowance beyond the points for joining, either to a plain strip or to another section of the "Seminole" patchwork.

Offset design using three colors

Cut two strips of fabric A, 1½-inches wide.

Cut two strips of fabric B, 1¼-inches wide.

Cut one strip of fabric C, 1¼-inches wide.

Stitch the strips together in the sequence illustrated. Press seams to one side.

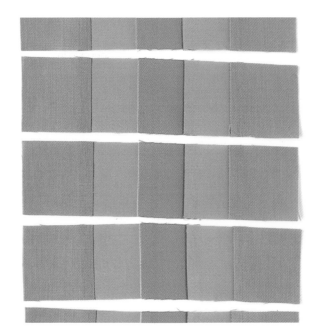

2 Cut into 1¼-inch sections across the seams.

3 Reposition the pieces so that the corners of fabric C will match up.

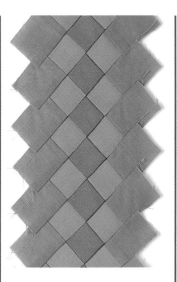

4 Stitch the pieces together and press seams to one side.

5 Trim away the points at the sides of the length, leaving ¼-inch beyond the corners of fabric A for seam allowance.

Angled design using two colors

1 Cut the two colors of fabric into different widths as follows: fabric A – two strips of 1½-inches, fabric B – one strip of ¾-inch. Seam together as illustrated. Straighten one short end, then measure 3 inches along from the top edge and cut at a slant.

2 Cut 2-inch sections along the strip parallel with the angled edge that you cut in step 1.

3 Seam these back together. Align the strips as shown, offsetting each narrow strip by ½-inch.

4 Press the seams and trim away the triangles at the sides, remembering to leave ¼-inch seam allowance.

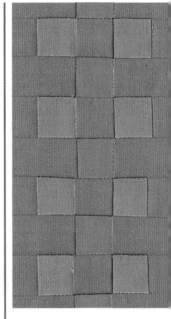

The designs above and below are made by combining different strip sequences or a set of strips with a plain color.

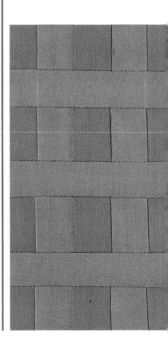

"STRING" PATCHWORK

This method of patchwork was devised to use up long strips of fabric – perhaps offcuts from dressmaking projects – which seem too narrow to be of any use at all. Seamed together and pressed flat, the strips result in pieces of patchwork that can be used as a single fabric to cut out the patches used to make up blocks. Choose a pattern that is simple to construct, and decide which of the pieces in the block are to be made of the "string" fabric. If necessary, make templates. Many of the simpler blocks can be cut out using the "Template-free" method. Before you begin, sort the fabrics to be used, and wash and press them. Fraying can be minimized by placing the pieces in a net bag.

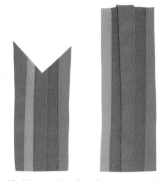

Making a "string" patchwork block

1 Cut strips of the same length in random widths between 1 and 3 inches.

If necessary, strips can be joined to increase lengths to that of the longest piece. Don't try to keep the strips of a consistent width; triangular or wedge-shaped pieces give finished blocks an interesting effect of movement.

2 Sew the strips together on the sewing machine, using a smaller stitch than normal to prevent seams from coming undone when patches are cut.

Press seams to one side on the back, and make sure that there are no small pleats between the seams by pressing again on the right side. If necessary, stitch strips to a foundation to stabilize flimsy fabrics.

3 Place strip A right side up, aligning raw edges with those of the foundation fabric. Then position the subsequent strips facedown against the preceding strip and stitch through the three layers (two strips and the foundation) taking ¼-inch seam allowance. Flip the strip over to reveal the right side, and press against the foundation. Continue until the foundation fabric is covered.

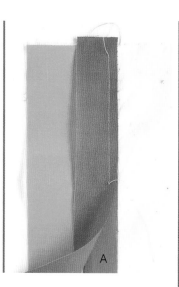

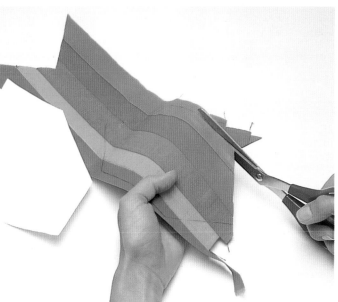

4 When you have created enough width to accommodate the template for your chosen block, cut out the patches and stitch the block together on the sewing machine. (See Joining pieced blocks).

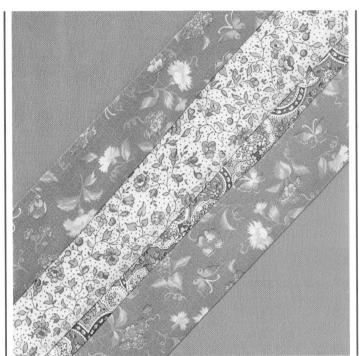

▲ This single patch from the **"Indian Hatchet"** design is set on a light background. It shows how different colors can create a totally different visual effect to the eight-block design opposite.

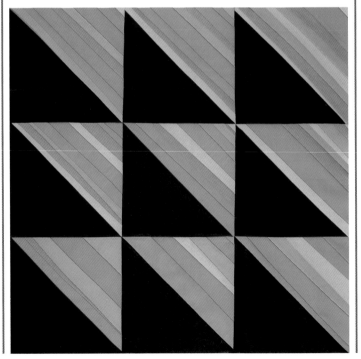

This **"Roman Stripe"** design (left) and **"Indian Hatchet"** (above right) use solid black to complement the "string" fabric.

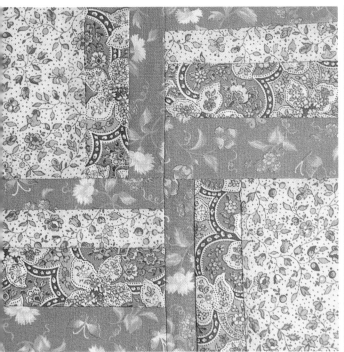

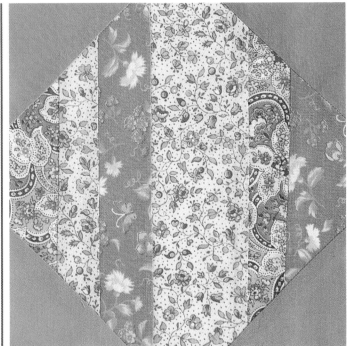

"Basket weave" (above left) and "Snowball" (above right) are also attractive examples of "string" patchwork.

"Railfence"
The "Railfence" block is very easy to piece and is similar in construction to the "Basketweave" block.

SPECIAL EFFECTS

If you want to add interest to the surface of a quilt there are various ways of creating texture by using three-dimensional sewing techniques or by fabric manipulation.

Piping is one design feature often used to highlight or to define particular areas of a quilt. It is especially interesting in pictorial quilts, where it can give depth and texture to a scene. "Wave Panels" have a similar illustrative function and can be made from different widths of fabric. Other decorations, such as "Suffolk Puffs" and "Prairie Points," also provide attractive and unusual additions to a quilt.

There are many imaginative and varied patchwork techniques which can be selected for an individual quilt, cushion or bed cover. Several of these, such as "Biscuit," "English" and "Folded Star" patchwork, are illustrated on the following pages.

Three-dimensional effects with fabric

The pliable nature of fabric makes it an ideal medium to create surface texture. By pleating, tucking or inserting additional details between seams, an extra dimension can be added to the surface of a quilt, making it worthy of close examination. These techniques, sometimes referred to as "fabric manipulation," can be used to provide focus areas or to emphasize the border in a geometric quilt. In pictorial quilts, a realistic appearance can be given to details by the use of special effects: try the "Wave Panel" to depict fields in a landscape, or "Prairie Points" as roof tiles in a house picture or the feathers on a bird.

Perhaps more familiar as a trim for upholstery and soft furnishings, piping can also be used effectively in patchwork projects. Fabric areas can be separated with a line of piping in a contrasting color, or it can be used as an additional frame around single blocks or the entire quilt, giving a crisp, defining line.

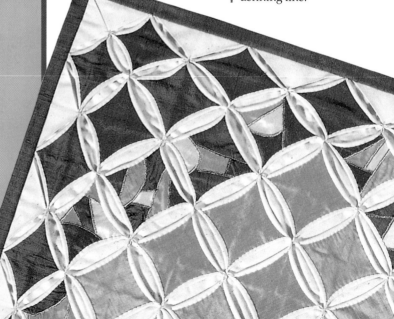

PIPING

Perhaps more familiar as a trim for upholstery and soft furnishings, piping can also be used very effectively in patchwork projects. As a finishing detail, for example, in the edges of cushions, it can also add individuality to any project. Fabric areas can be separated with a line of piping in a contrasting color, or it can be used as an additional frame around single blocks or the entire quilt, giving a crisp defining line. Piping is often used to outline individual features such as doorways, garden arches or fields to place emphasis on chosen areas.

Daphne Ramsey,
Cathedral Window Wall Hanging.
This quilt combines a variation on the "Cathedral Window" technique and machine-embroidered "crazy" patchwork.

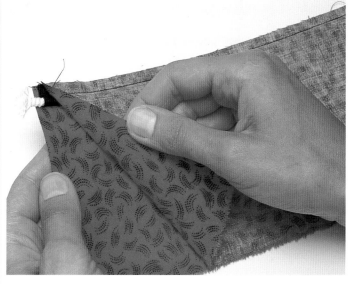

1 The most defined piping can be made by using piping cord. The piping itself should be cut into strips of 1 inch or wider, and folded in half to enclose the cord. The piping and cord should then be seamed into the separate fabric areas as shown.

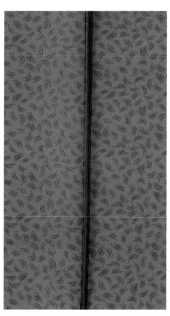

2 When the material is opened out, the cord within the piping is clearly defined.

3 Alternatively, simply sew the folded strip of piping into the seam and stitch, using a ¼ inch seam allowance.

4 Curved piping can be produced by cutting bias strips (see page 109) to create the effect shown above.

"WAVE PANEL" AND "PRAIRIE POINTS"

The effect achieved by this technique belies its simplicity of construction. Folded strips of fabric are inserted between seams in the background, then stitched up and down in opposing direction to give the "Wave" effect. A dark/light contrast between background and folded strips gives a pleasing result which could be used as the center panel for a cushion or bag. Toning colors might be used, for instance, a combination of greens, to create realistic areas such as a plowed field in a pictorial quilt. Experiment with different widths for both the backing and folded strips; a very narrow series of strips will appear flatter, while wider ones will stand away from the background, giving a more three-dimensional effect.

1 The tucks are cut and folded lengthwise, before being inserted and stitched into the seams with which the background strips are joined. Cut the "tuck" fabric marginally narrower than the background strips, e.g., for background strips of 1¼ inches, cut tucks 1 inch wide. Fold the tucks in half lengthwise, right sides together, and press.

2 Place the long edges of the background strips right sides together, with the tucks between them. Seam the background strips together, trapping the tucks in the ¼-inch seam allowance, so that all four, raw edges are together.

3 Press all the seams on the back in the same direction.

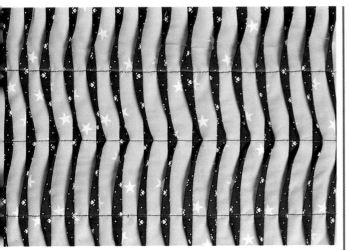

Prairie points

These small folded triangles can be used to add accent, color or surface interest.

4 On the right side, stitch the tucks against the background down the center of the panel, then press them in the opposite direction on each side of the line, and stitch down to the background again to create the wave effect.

Continue to stitch the tucks up and down until the whole panel is completed.

1 Fold a square of fabric in half to create a rectangle, then fold the corners across to make the triangle. All raw edges will now be together on the longest side of the triangle. Press well to form sharp creases.

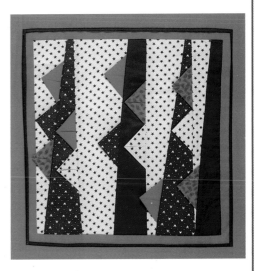

Alternatives

5 A similar effect can be created by stitching pin tucks into the fabric rather than inserting the tucks. There will be no dark/light contrast, only the effect of shadow created by the way light falls on the fabric.

6 Pinch the pin tucks together at regular alternating intervals for a "smocked" effect.

2 Insert the resulting triangle between two pieces of fabric in the seam allowance (so that all raw edges are together). Stitch, trapping the triangle in the seam.

3 In this panel, prairie points are trapped between wedge-shaped strips of fabric. The double border has a folded strip of piping inserted between the two strips to add a narrow, contrasting line.

"SUFFOLK PUFFS"

Also known as "Yo-yo," this technique was used to make light bed throws from scrap fabrics in the 1920s and 30s. Circles of fabric are gathered, and the thread is pulled up tightly to create medallion shapes. These are caught together at a point on each side, leaving spaces between which give a decorative, lace-like effect. The best fabric to use is fine lightweight cotton with a close weave, which does not easily fray and will allow the gathering thread to be pulled up tightly.

1 Decide on the size of the finished "Yo-yo" unit and cut a circle of fabric twice this size. A piece 4½ inches in diameter will give a finished unit of 2¼ inches.

2 Turn a narrow single hem on the cut circle of fabric. An easy way to make an even hem on the fabric is to baste it over a circle of paper, turning the seam allowance over the paper in the same way as for "English" patchwork. Press the fabric circle with the paper inside it, then remove the basting and paper. The turning will be firmly and evenly creased, and the circle will be the size of the paper shape.

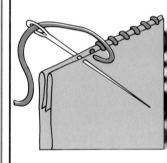

Whipping stitch
Whipping stitch, also called oversewing, is used instead of slipstitch to join two folded edges of fabric when a strong joining is needed. It is an ideal stitch for joining the circles together, see step 4 right.

3 Using thread to match the fabric, doubled if necessary to take the strain of pulling up the gathers, work a ring of running stitches around the outer edges of the circle. Leave a long knotted end at the beginning of the work.

4 When the circle of stitches is complete, pull the thread tightly from both ends to gather up the fabric. Make the opening as small as possible by pulling the gathers closely. Knot the thread ends together, and stitch them out of sight. Flatten the fabric circle with the opening in the center and steam-press. Make as many units as necessary for the project.

Join the units together with four or five whipstitches at a point on each side of the units, matching the folds together. Neaten the thread ends.

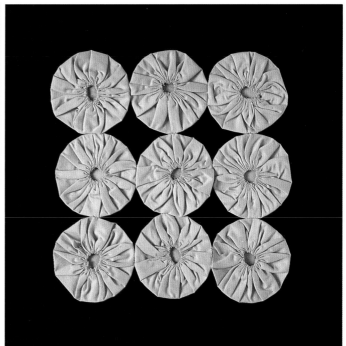

6 If a more solid appearance is required, the project can be mounted and appliquéd onto another fabric.

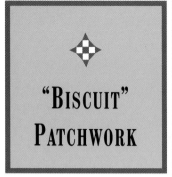

"BISCUIT" PATCHWORK

This rather novel method of patchwork makes a very light, warm form of cot or bed cover. Patches in multiples of a single shape, usually squares, are made into pockets and filled with batting. These individual pouches are then sewn together to create a textured surface of raised squares separated by the joining channels. No quilting is necessary as the separate areas are complete units which hold the batting in place, preventing it from migrating. Designs for "biscuit" quilts can be adapted from any traditional designs which are made up of squares; "Trip Around the World," "Irish Chain" or even a simple nine-patch are all suitable. This would also be an ideal project for a scrap or charm quilt.

1 Each of the "biscuits" is made by sewing a larger top square onto a base. Preshrunk cotton in a light color is a suitable fabric for the base squares. Decide what size to make the unit, and cut base squares to this measurement plus ½ in for seam allowances. Cut the top squares 1 to 1½ inches larger than the base. A bigger difference in the size between the top square and the base will result in a fatter pouch, and thus a thicker quilt overall.

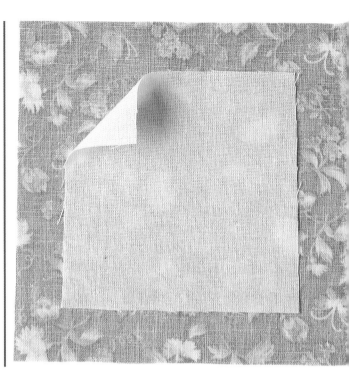

2 Place the larger square on top of the base, wrong sides facing, and pin the corners together. Then pleat the sides of the top square evenly, and stitch the two layers together on three sides by hand or machine.

Stitch inside the seam allowance so that these stitches will be concealed when the "biscuit" units are joined together.

3 Push loose batting into the open side of each piece, using the same amount for each square. Pin the opening, and stitch the two layers together, pleating the top square in the same way as on the other three sides to enclose the batting.

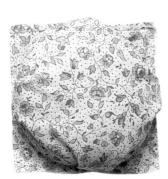

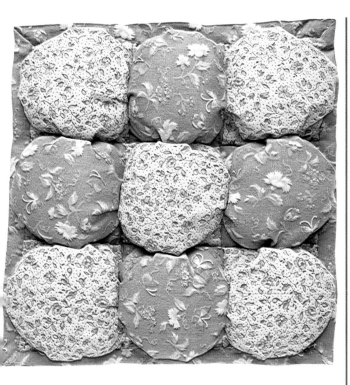

4 Make enough units to complete your project. Stitch them together by hand or machine, taking ¼-inch seam allowance. Finger-press the seams open or to one side on the back. They should not be ironed as this may damage the batting.

5 To conceal the seams on the back, line the completed "biscuit" top with a piece of harmonizing fabric, finishing the edges with binding or by turning the edges together (see page 105 for finishing techniques). The quilt top and backing fabric can be secured together with stitches or knots at regular intervals between the "biscuit" units.

"FOLDED STAR" PATCHWORK

Rectangles of fabric folded into small triangles make these crisp star medallions, which can be incorporated into quilts or used as centers for cushions and smaller items. When selecting fabric for "Folded Star," look for pure cotton which creases well, and choose a color scheme with sharp contrasts. Plain colors or small prints are the most effective; larger prints will not work as well when folded into small units. The medallions are worked from the center – each round of triangles held down at the point and stitched to a foundation square. The folding and overlapping produces quite a thickness of fabric, so it is not practical to quilt it.

1 Cut a square of foundation fabric larger than the finished size of the medallion by about 2 inches all around. To make the triangles, cut a strip of fabric 1½ inches wide across the fabric from selvedge to selvedge. Fold down a ¼-inch hem along one long edge. Cut this strip into 2½-inch pieces.

Fold these pieces in half to find the center, then fold the corners down to create triangles and steam-press.

2 Round 1: press the foundation fabric to form creases vertically, horizontally and diagonally and arrange the first four triangles, folded sides on top, in the center with the points just touching. The angled sides should be in line with the diagonal creases.

Secure the points to the foundation fabric with a stitch, and, if the fabric frays easily, use overcasting or baste around the outer edge of the triangles. Trim off the corners to reduce bulk.

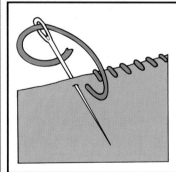

Overcasting
Overcasting is used to finish the edges of fabrics that fray easily. Work from either direction, taking the thread over the edge of the fabric. Do not pull the thread too tightly, or the edges of the fabric will curl and make bulges.

5 Round 4: make sixteen triangles. Position eight of these ½ inch back from the points of round 3, then place the other eight with points just touching the star points of round 2. Stitch down the points and round the outer edges as before. Trim away the triangle corners.

Further rounds require sixteen triangles. Continue to build the star outward setting the triangles back by ½ inch on each round until the star is the desired size.

3 Round 2: with contrasting fabric make eight triangles. Position the points ½ inch away from the center, and stitch to the foundation through the triangles on round 1, catching the points down with a stitch and basting around the outer edges. Trim the corners.

4 Round 3: make eight triangles to contrast with the previous round and position these ½ inch back from the points of round 2. Stitch down the points and baste round the outer edges as before. Trim the corners.

Framing the star
To set the star into a circular frame, cut two pieces of fabric to the correct size, plus seam allowances. One is for the frame and one for a facing. For a 10-inch-square frame cut two 10½-inch squares. Press and pin them right sides together. Measure the circle for the "window" and mark this in the center of the squares. Stitch round the circle, then cut out the center, leaving ¼-inch seam allowance. Clip all round the seam allowance just short of the stitching line, then turn the facing to the inside and press. The two fabrics are now right-sides out. Position the frame over the medallion, pin, and stitch round. Trim the square to size, and baste the three layers together. The bottom layer is the calico backing of the star.

"CATHEDRAL WINDOW"

This technique uses squares of folded fabric as a background to show off small "windows" of decorative fabric. The preparation of the background squares reduces them in size by just over half, so allow about 2¼ times the finished size of the foundation fabric. The size of the squares is flexible, but 6 or 7 inches, which results in a window about 2-inches square, is a popular size. Experiment with different fabrics – a striped background fabric gives an interesting effect. Windows can be made with floral or shiny fabric. Alternatively, contrast a patterned background with plain inserts.

The foundation squares can be prepared by hand or machine.

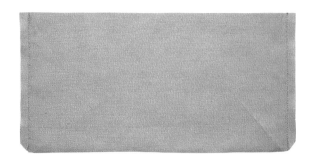

By hand
1 Cut a square of foundation fabric and turn a small single hem (about ¼-inch) all round. Press flat.

Fold the corners to the center, pin down and press well to give a sharp crease.

By machine
1 Cut the square of foundation fabric, fold in half and press. Stitch up the two short sides, taking a ¼-inch seam allowance. Clip the corners off the seams on the folded side and press seams open.

2 Pull the open edge apart so that the two seam ends meet.

2 Repeat step 1, folding corners to the center, then fasten these down through all layers with one or two small cross-stitches.

3 Stitch across this opening, leaving a gap to turn the square through to the right side.

4 Clip the corners off this seam at each end, and press seams open. Turn through the gap right side out, poke out the corners and press.

5 Fold the corners to the center and secure through all layers with cross-stitches as for the hand-stitched method.

Joining the squares

Whichever way you have prepared the squares, the procedure is the same from now on.

1 When you have prepared enough foundation squares, place them right sides together. Join along one edge with whipstitch from corner to corner.

2 Join as many squares as you need for your design into a block. As squares are joined, the area into which the "window" will be stitched is created. This is a smaller square set as a diamond "on point." Measure this area and cut pieces of decorative fabric for inserts.

3 To add the decorative panels, pin them in position and curl the folded edges over, then hem down in a smooth curve, using thread that matches the foundation fabric.

4 Repeat until all the window spaces are filled. To fill the triangular shapes at the edges, fold the decorative squares in half diagonally, and pin them in position. Then hem the two curved edges down and slipstitch the folds together along the outer edge.

"Cathedral Window"

"Crazy" Patchwork

The "Crazy" block uses shapes that fit together in an irregular but economical way. The jigsaw-like construction allowed for the use of every available scrap of fabric, wasting none of what was once a valuable resource.

By the last quarter of the 19th century the "crazy" quilt was transformed into a "throw" made of rich fabrics such as silk, velvet and taffeta, and often embellished with sentimental mementoes, lavish embroidery, lace and ribbons. The only similarity between these Victorian "crazy" quilts and their predecessors was their randomly cut shapes.

"Crazy" quilt patches are stitched onto squares of foundation fabric so no batting is necessary. There are various ways of constructing a block.

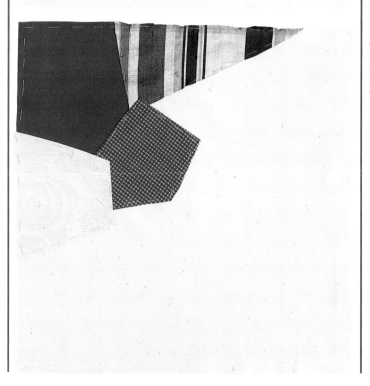

Method 1

1 Start with a foundation square of white sheeting or similar weight fabric which measures 10 to 14 inches square. Position the first patch in one corner, and pin it down securely.

2 Work across from the corner, pinning down further pieces and overlapping the edges by about ¼ to ½ inch to fit them together like a jigsaw.

When the foundation square is covered, turn under the overlapping raw edges and paste down the pieces to the foundation. Leave raw edges around the outside of the square – these will be contained by the seams when the blocks are joined together.

Embroider over the edges where the patches overlap and meet. Ribbons, lace, fragments of embroidery, and old buttons or beads, etc. can be applied into the patches.
Trim the completed squares to the same size and join them together with a ¼ inch seam allowance, stitching through all layers. If preferred the blocks can be separated by sashing strips.

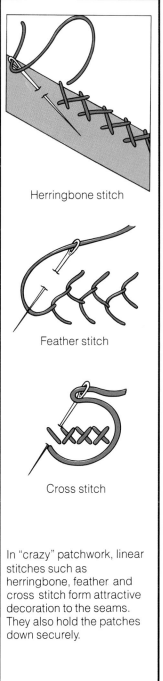

Herringbone stitch

Feather stitch

Cross stitch

In "crazy" patchwork, linear stitches such as herringbone, feather and cross stitch form attractive decoration to the seams. They also hold the patches down securely.

Method 2
In this method the block is built outward around a center patch. Prepare the foundation square as for method 1 and select a piece of interesting fabric for the center patch.

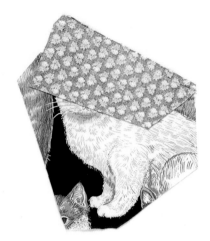

1 Cut out a four- or five-sided shape, and put this right side up in the center on top of the foundation. Press lightly and pin down.

2 Select a second fabric and cut a random straight-sided piece. Place this right-side down, aligning one straight edge against one side of the first patch. Stitch by hand or machine through the two layers and the foundation fabric, using a running stitch and taking ¼ inch seam allowance

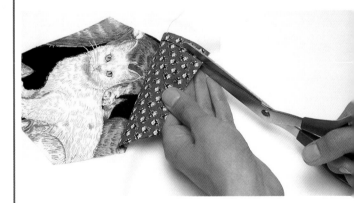

3 Flip patch 2 over to reveal the right side of the fabric and trim so that the straight edges of patch 1 extend along the edges of patch 2 .

4 Add further patches right-side down along the straight edges created as you stitch and flip them over.

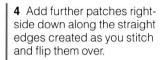

5 Continue until the foundation square is completely covered. Trim the square and press.

6 The blocks can be joined edge to edge, as illustrated here in "Cat Crazy," or separated with sashing strips. This quilt is machine-quilted.

APPLIQUE

In the technique of appliqué, pieces of fabric are cut out and stitched onto a foundation. Originally developed as a means of extending the life of a garment or bedspread, or of making expensive materials go further, its potential as a medium for decorative and pictorial designs in fabric was soon realized and exploited. Because curved shapes can be more easily used than in pieced patchwork, elaborate designs using motifs such as flowers, birds and fruit became a way of showing off the skills of needlewomen in the 19th century. Baltimore brides' quilts, made of elaborately appliquéd blocks containing floral and patriotic elements, are fine examples of this technique.

Katharine Guerrier,
Fruit Basket Block.
This block combines patchwork and machine-appliqué techniques. Final details are added with machine-embroidery.

DESIGNING FOR HAND-APPLIQUE

MACHINE APPLIQUE

REVERSE APPLIQUE

"APPLIQUE PERSE"

SHADOW APPLIQUE

HAWAIIAN APPLIQUE

"STAINED GLASS" APPLIQUE

DESIGNING FOR HAND-APPLIQUE

When the separate pieces of an appliqué design are stitched down by hand, the raw edges of the fabrics must be turned under to prevent fraying before being hemmed to the foundation. When designing for hand appliqué, bear this in mind and try to strike a balance between shapes which are so simple that they look crude, and those which have such elaborate curves that difficulties may occur in stitching down the edges. Sketch out a few ideas using the outline shapes of leaves, petals or fruit. Appliqué can be used to create one large single image such as the "Tree of Life" designs, but for a first project try a smaller panel which may be the beginning of a repeat block quilt or could be made into a cushion.

Hand-appliqué

1 When you are satisfied with your design, decide on the number of templates required, and trace each shape from the drawing.

2 From the traced shapes make full-size templates from thin card.

3 Cut a piece of foundation fabric allowing 2 inches extra or so all round for turnings. Using the templates to draw each shape, copy the design onto the foundation fabric. It may be advisable to use a fabric marker which can be erased. This is in case your appliqué shapes do not quite cover the lines.

Making bias strips
To achieve a consistent width which lies flat and will curve smoothly, make a bias tube which cuts out the need to turn under a seam allowance as you stitch. A 10 to 11 inch-square of fabric will make enough strips to make stems for one block. Begin with a true bias by folding the fabric diagonally, making a 45-degree angle. Press a crease on the fold line and cut along this crease. From the resulting triangle cut 1-inch-wide bias strips. Fold a strip in half lengthwise, wrong sides together. With the folded edge next to the presser foot of your sewing machine, stitch a narrow tube. Trim away excess seam allowance. Roll the tube so that the seam lies down the

center and press flat. A bias press bar will make this process easier. This is a narrow, flat piece of metal or heat-resistant nylon which can be pushed into the tube, making it easier to maneuver the seam to the flat of the bar and press it with a hot iron. Remove the bar and press again. If your design

calls for narrower stems than can be made using this method, cut bias strips ½ or ¾ inch wide, then overlap one long edge over the other one, making a narrow strip. Baste the edges to hold them in place making sure the width of the strip is consistent.

4 To make stems and vines (which are often the first pieces to be stitched down), make bias strips as described. Place the stems in position on the foundation, then pin and stitch them in place, concealing the seam or the fold at the back.

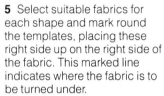

5 Select suitable fabrics for each shape and mark round the templates, placing these right side up on the right side of the fabric. This marked line indicates where the fabric is to be turned under.

Mark and cut out the patch, allowing up to ¼ inch turning, clip concave curves within the turning (no more than ⅛ inch), then fold under the raw edges on the line marked round the template.

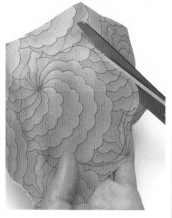

6 The clipped concave curves will fan out as they are turned under. Fabric may have to be folded twice on sharp points in order to reduce bulk, so trim away as much as you can from the point without cutting too close to the drawn line.

7 For inside points, clip into the point and fold under the turning, being careful not to allow fraying at the inner point. Baste to hold the turnings in place until the piece is stitched to the foundation.

Building up the design

1 Many appliqué patterns have shapes that overlap. Begin with the shapes that lie partially underneath. The raw edges which will be covered do not need to be turned under. Build up the design, using a logical sequence to stitch down the shapes. Where several layers are stitched down on top of each other, cut away the foundation fabric from behind, ¼ inch in from the stitching line to reduce bulk. Press appliqué on a thick pad such as a towel to prevent it from being flattened.

2 Embroidered details can be added when the design is complete. Assemble the appliqué block or quilt top with the batting and backing, and quilt the background and around the appliqué shapes.

Using freezer paper
For each fabric shape, cut out a corresponding piece of freezer paper. Place this paper on the wrong side of the patch with the waxed side of the paper uppermost. Clip curves as before, then fold over the turning onto the waxed side of the paper (above left). Press down the turnings with a dry iron. The fabric will stick to and be shaped by the paper (above right). Stitch the patch in position. To remove the paper, leave a gap to detach it gently and pull it through before closing the seam, or cut away the foundation from behind the patch ¼ inch from the stitching line and pull it out from the back.

Appliqué shapes can also be formed by basting them onto papers cut to the shape of the desired patch, then pressing them to form a crease around the outer edge. Remove the basting stitches and the paper before sewing the shape down.

Hemming stitch
Using a single strand of thread to match the patch, sew the shapes to the background with a neat hemming stitch. Make sure that the needle goes straight down from the fold of the fabric into the background and comes up about ¼ inch farther along into the fold. For a more visible, decorative stitch, appliqué can be stitched down with a small running stitch. A special needle designed to help make small, neat stitches has been developed for appliqué.

MACHINE APPLIQUE

If you have a sewing machine which will do an even, close satin stitch – the same stitch that is used for buttonholes – then you will be able to work appliqué panels by machine. The satin stitch is used to stitch down the shapes and cover the raw edges simultaneously, so no seam allowances are necessary. When designing panels for machine appliqué, begin with simple shapes which can be easily guided through the sewing machine without too many sharp turns. Flowers, fruit and leaf shapes can provide inspiration when designing appliqué panels. Sketch out a few ideas before starting to cut fabric.

1 When you have worked out a design, decide whether it is necessary to make templates; simple shapes may be cut freehand. Trace more complicated shapes from your drawing and make templates from thin cardboard.

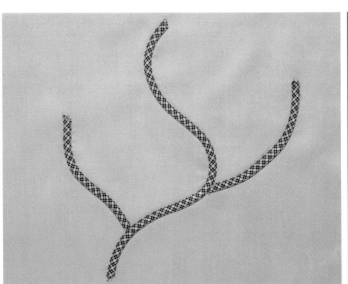

2 Cut a piece of fabric for the background slightly larger than the desired finished size, and begin by stitching the preliminary details such as stems (made as described in "Hand-appliqué") using a machine-straight stitch. If you are adding appliqué to a patchwork block, you should assemble the patchwork block first.

3 Choose fabrics appropriate to your design, and press well to remove all creases. When stitching appliqué shapes by machine, the background has tendency to pucker. To avoid this, use a paper-backed fusible web. Place this against the wrong side of the appliqué fabric with the glue side, which feels slightly rougher than the paper side, down. Iron to the fabric with a medium heat.

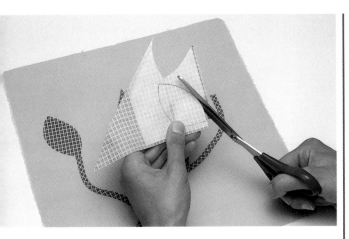

Appliqué shapes can be drawn on paper freehand, or you can draw around templates made from your design. Cut out the appliqué shapes and the paper together, then peel away the paper.

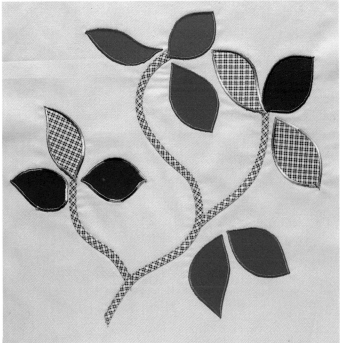

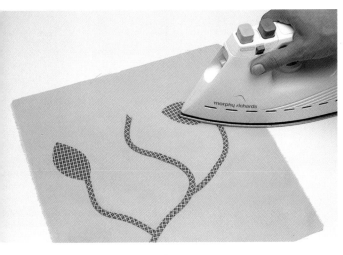

Position the appliqué shape onto the background and press with a medium iron to fuse. The use of paper-backed fusible web will slightly stiffen the fabric. If you want your panel to remain soft, cut out the appliqué from fabric, place it in position on the background and baste it down.

6 When all the appliqué shapes are in position, set the machine to the correct stitch. If you are *not* using paper-backed fusible web, stitch round the appliqué shape first with a straight stitch or open zigzag stitch to hold it, then set the stitch to a close satin stitch. Loosen the top tension slightly, if you can, to prevent the bottom thread from showing on the top. Guide the shapes through the machine, turning to follow the curves. If you can, vary the width of the zigzag as you go. Try narrowing it to a point for leaf tips, or widening it to make more rounded curves. Variegated machine embroidery threads give an interesting effect around the edges of the appliqué shapes.

7 Extra machine-stitched details, such as on the edges of the leaves can be added.

REVERSE APPLIQUE

Reverse appliqué is done by placing two or more layers of fabric together, and then cutting away upper layers in a design. When it is worked by hand, the raw edges of the fabric must be turned under to neaten them. Choose finely woven, pure cotton fabrics that will not easily fray for reverse appliqué; when turning the fabric under in curves and sharp inner corners, the fabric has to be clipped, and this may create a weak point at which a coarsely woven fabric will fray.

The same principles apply to reverse appliqué by machine or by hand: fabric is layered and stitched together, and the upper layers are cut away to reveal the design. The difference is that no turnings need to be made when sewing by machine, as the shapes are stitched together with a close satin stitch that holds down the fabrics and seals the raw edges simultaneously.

Hand reverse appliqué

1 Cut two pieces of fabric in the desired finished size of the work, allowing 1 inch or so extra around the outer edge for turnings. Press them together, placing the right side of the lower fabric against the wrong side of the upper one. Draw the design onto the top fabric, then baste all round the outer edge of it, just over ½ inch away.

2 Using a small, sharp pair of scissors, cut away the top fabric ¼ inch inside the drawn line. Clip any concave curves and inner corners towards, and just inside, the drawn line.

3 Select thread which matches the top fabric. Turning under the raw edges on the drawn line as you go, slipstitch the top layer of fabric to the one underneath. Use small, neat stitches and turn the edge under with the point of your needle, holding it in place with your thumb just ahead of your stitching. At sharp inner corners place two or three stitches close together to prevent fraying.

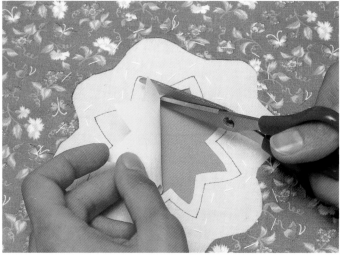

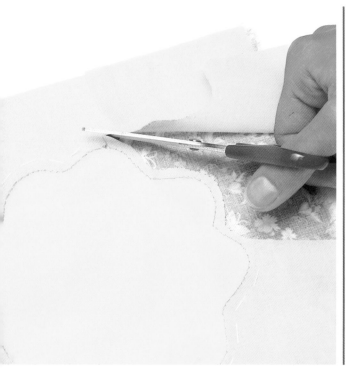

5 For a third color draw a second shape onto the appliqué fabric. Cut the third fabric slightly larger than this shape and pin it behind the drawing on the front. Baste round the drawing as in step 1, then cut away the new shape and hem down. Use thread to match the second color.

The edges of the two layers of fabric can be tacked together around the outside of the piece, or excess fabric from the top layer could be trimmed away ¼ inch from your stitching if preferred. This will serve to reduce bulk on the finished piece.

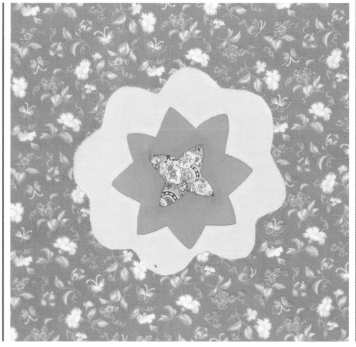

6 More shapes can be added, building up the design from three or four colors. Press reverse appliqué on a thick pad such as a towel to prevent it from becoming too flattened.

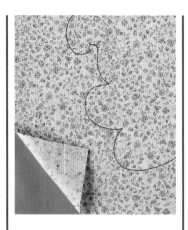

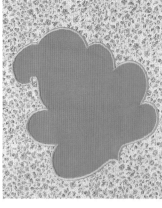

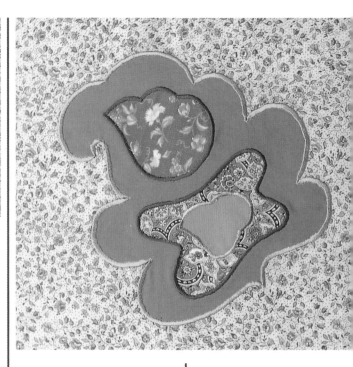

Machine reverse appliqué

1 Cut two squares of fabric in the desired size, remembering to allow extra fabric for turnings. Place them both right side up, one on top of the other, and steam-press. Pin or baste them together. Draw the design to be appliquéd on the top fabric, then stitch around the drawn line with a straight stitch.

3 Set the machine to a close satin stitch (buttonhole stitch) and sew around the shape, covering the raw edges and stitching the top and bottom layers together. Satin stitch has a tendency to pucker the fabric. To prevent this, baste a piece of thin paper underneath the design to be stitched, which can be torn away afterwards.

5 The design can be built up by drawing further shapes on the area of the appliqué. Cut pieces of fabric slightly larger than the area of the drawing, and baste them to the back, behind the drawn shape. Straight stitch round the drawn line, then repeat steps 2 and 3. As you progress, trim away excess fabrics outside the stitching line on the back to reduce bulk.

2 With a small, sharp pair of scissors, carefully cut away the top layer inside the line and close to the stitching, being careful not to cut the underneath layer as well.

4 Trim away the excess base fabric on the back, outside the area of the appliqué and about ¼ inch away from the stitching line.

Mola appliqué

An elaborate form of reverse appliqué, molas are made by the Kuna Indians from the San Blas islands of Panama. Panels are made to decorate the front and back panels of the traditional blouses they call the "mola," still largely worn as everyday clothing by the women and girls. When the government of Panama tried to prohibit the wearing of molas during an attempt to integrate the island populations, the move was met with resistance, and molas continued to be worn as an expression of pride and independence. Designs worked on molas record plant and animal life, scenes from local ceremonies and religious lore, and even contemporary events. Up to four layers are worked in fine stitching with narrow channels, more colors being added by smaller pieces which are inserted in strategic positions. Final details are embroidered on.

Pa Ndau cushion cover.
Pa Ndau designs and Molas are becoming highly collectible.

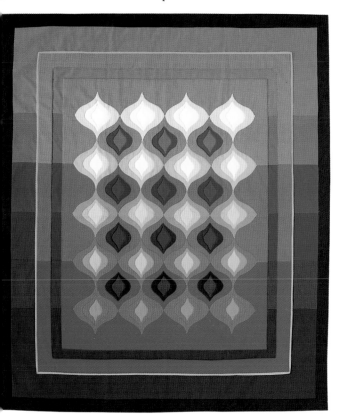

Ann Tuck,
Yayacca.
A three-layer Mola quilt using traditional appliqué techniques. The design lines were worked by stitching through from the back of the basic fabric onto the middle layer, which was then cut and hemmed down. The third layer was worked in the same way.

Pa Ndau

Pa Ndau is another form of complex reverse appliqué made by the Hmong hill tribes of Southeast Asia. Geometric shapes abstracted from natural forms such as snails, spider's webs, stars and elephants, have symbolic meanings and are worked on two or three layers of fabric. The resulting panels are used to decorate clothing and household textiles. As with molas, embroidery is used to embellish the designs.

"APPLIQUE PERSE"

"Appliqué Perse" or "Broderie Perse" is a technique of cutting motifs from printed fabrics, and rearranging them on a plain background before stitching them down. Originally a means of making rare and expensive fabrics go further, or preserving the life of a partly worn piece, it became very popular in England in the 18th century and later in America. Fabrics imported from India were block-printed with flora and fauna and brightly colored, sometimes by hand. Despite attempts by the British textile industry to ban the import of these fabrics, their popularity was such that designs were copied from English embroideries to cater to British tastes. Their scarcity, largely due to the law which was passed in 1721 banning their use on clothing or household furnishings, increased the popularity of "Broderie Perse" as the technique could be used to make small amounts of the fabric go further. "Broderie Perse" can be done in the traditional way – by hand – or the technique can be updated by using machine-appliqué.

Choosing fabrics

When choosing suitable fabrics for "Broderie Perse," look for those with clearly defined motifs such as flowers, birds, animals, etc. Select those which can be cut out fairly simply. Fine stems and other small details are best added as surface embroidery later.

By hand

If working by hand, cut out the motifs, allowing ¼ to ½ inch extra for turnings. Prepare the pieces by turning under the raw edges in any of the methods described as for hand-appliqué (see pages 85–87). Arrange them on a plain background. Pin down, and stitch as for hand appliqué. Add further details to the pieces with embroidery.

By machine

If sewing the motifs down by machine, cut them out with a narrow outline; remember that machine satin stitch takes up a width of about ⅛ inch. Arrange them onto the background, and baste them in position, then stitch round the edges with a close satin stitch. Try using decorative thread as an embellishment. Use machine-embroidery to add fine details.

SHADOW APPLIQUE

In this appliqué technique the patches which make up the design are trapped between two layers of fabric. A light-colored plain fabric such as cream or white cotton is best for the base. The top fabric must be transparent so that the design shows through: organza, chiffon or a close net would be suitable. The two layers are stitched together around each of the appliqué shapes with a running stitch which holds the design in position. No seam allowance is necessary as there are no turnings made on the appliqué.

1 Cut out appliqué shapes according to your chosen design. Use strong, plain colors, as the sheer top layer gives the fabrics a muted effect. As with machine-appliqué, if you are using fairly simple shapes, appliqués can be cut freehand. Whether or not you are using templates, do not add seam allowance. A light coating of spray starch will prevent the edges from fraying.

2 Arrange the design on the foundation fabric, using a small dab of fabric glue to hold pieces in position.

3 Smooth the sheer fabric over the top of the appliqués. Pin and baste the layers together around the design and the outer edges.

4 Using thread which blends with the top layer of fabric, stitch around each of the appliqué shapes with a running stitch. Details such as leaf veins and stems can be embroidered on top with a contrasting embroidery thread.

HAWAIIAN APPLIQUE

Patchwork and quilting were first introduced to the Hawaiian islanders by missionaries who started to go there in the early 19th century. A unique design style, consisting of a large appliqué called a "Kapa Lau" which was stitched to the foundation fabric, developed. This was designed much in the same way that paper snowflakes are cut – the top fabric is folded and cut in layers. Shapes which inspired the designs were taken from everyday things such as flowers, leaves and fruit. Individual designs were jealously guarded; it was considered wrong to copy another person's design. Hawaiian quilts are traditionally made in two bright plain colors, usually red or blue on white. The appliqué covers most of the background, which can be as big as a full-size bedspread or as small as a cushion. The quilting, known as "echo" or "wave" quilting, follows the shape of the appliqué and radiates out in lines rather like ripples across the background to the edges of the piece. In Hawaii this method of quilting is called "Luma Lau."

1 Try out folded paper designs before making a final choice. Fold paper squares in half, then into quarters, and finally once more into eighths. Draw and cut the design between the two folded edges, which should remain uncut. Open out the paper, and check the designs until you have a satisfactory one. Cut out a one-eighth segment to use as a template.

2 Cut two squares of fabric 2 inches or so larger than the paper pattern, one for the background and one for the appliqué. Fold each one in half and in half again, ironing the creases and making sure the grain runs straight with the folds. Finally, fold diagonally, pressing again. Pin the paper template onto the appliqué fabric, and mark around the shape. Remove the paper, and pin the fabric layers back together. Cut out the appliqué with a pair of sharp scissors, making sure that the layers do not shift.

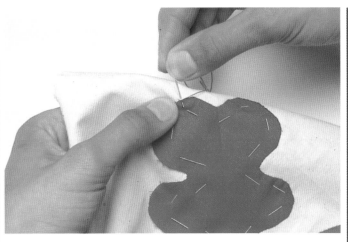

4 Starting near the center and turning under the raw edges of the appliqué with the point of the needle as you go, slip-hem the appliqué shape, using thread to match. When there is a sharp inner turn, make several stitches to prevent fraying. To stitch points, work up to the tip, then tuck under the fabric on the other side with the needle and continue. Always use small close stitches.

Unfold the background fabric, and smooth it out on a flat surface. Remove the pins from the appliqué, unfold it and position it onto the background, lining up the creases and pinning the two layers together. Work from the center outward and smooth as you go. Baste all around the shape ³⁄₈ inch from the edges.

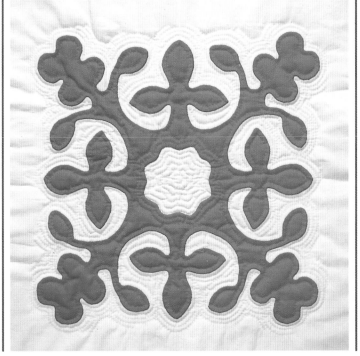

5 To quilt, assemble the top, batting and backing and baste the three layers together. Quilt, echoing the shapes of the appliqué in lines about ½ inch apart.

"STAINED GLASS" APPLIQUE

"Stained Glass" appliqué is a relatively recent form, which uses bold shapes outlined with narrow black lines to resemble stained glass. The fabric pieces are cut out, and arranged on a square of foundation fabric edge to edge, rather like the pieces of a jigsaw puzzle. The raw edges of the fabric shapes are then covered with bias strips which imitate the leading in a stained glass window. When designing for this technique, use simple shapes with gentle curves. Each drawn line must either connect to another or go to the edge of the design, just like in real stained glass. Avoid very small shapes – curving the bias strips which form the separating "leading" is too difficult. For design ideas, look at stylized drawings in children's books or large print fabrics and wallpapers with distinct linear designs. Wrought iron railings, or even real stained glass windows, can be a source of inspiration for the more ambitious needleworker.

1 On good quality sketching paper, make a drawing which will be the full size of the completed panel. Trace the drawing, then on the other side of the tracing paper mark all the lines with an embroidery transfer pencil. For the foundation, cut a piece of light-colored cotton or calico slightly larger than the finished size of the panel. Transfer the design onto the foundation fabric with a hot dry iron.

2 Number each shape on the drawing and the tracing, then cut up the drawing to use as templates. The numbered tracing is your guide to the design. Do not add any seam allowances.

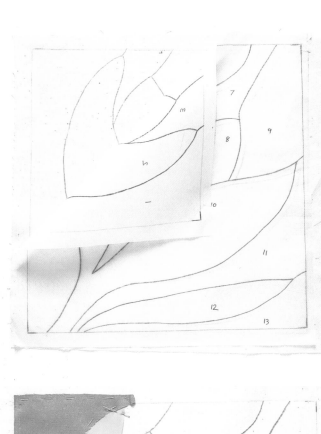

3 Use the templates to cut out fabric shapes. Tack them onto the foundation around the edges of each shape, placing the shapes edge to edge on the transferred design.

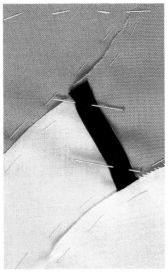

5 Place the bias tape along the edges of the shapes, centering it so that all raw edges are covered. Pin in place carefully.

6 Study the design to decide which strips to apply first – those which run into a continuing line must be tucked under and stitched down.

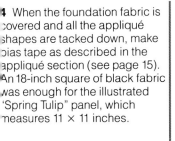

4 When the foundation fabric is covered and all the appliqué shapes are tacked down, make bias tape as described in the appliqué section (see page 15). An 18-inch square of black fabric was enough for the illustrated 'Spring Tulip" panel, which measures 11 × 11 inches.

7 Slip-hem the bias tape down along both edges with a thread to match the tape. Work the inner edges of the curves first, then the outer edges. Remove all basting stitches before adding a border.

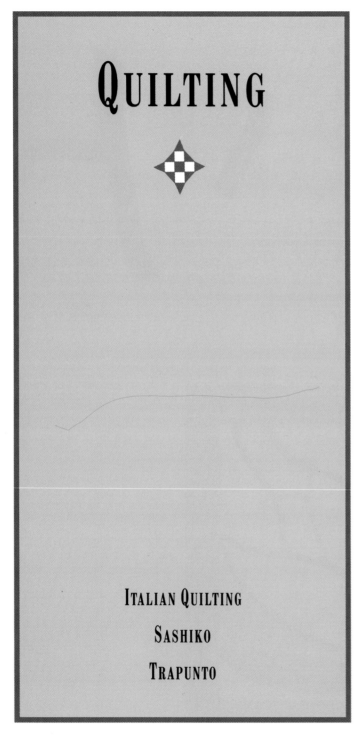

QUILTING

ITALIAN QUILTING

SASHIKO

TRAPUNTO

ITALIAN QUILTING

Wool or cord threaded through stitched channels forms a raised, linear design in the technique of Italian or corded quilting. It was used as a form of decoration on quilts and clothing as early as the 17th and 18th centuries and enjoyed a revival in the 1930s and 40s. Corded quilting is more decorative than practical; it cannot be padded and this is one possible explanation of its name – Italian quilting – where warmer bedcovers were not so necessary in the Mediterranean climate. Light-colored fabrics are most suitable for projects in Italian quilting as they show off the sculptured effect more easily. Designs can be adapted from various sources; plant forms, celtic knots, hearts and circles, for example, could all be starting points.

1 Plan your design, and make the necessary templates. Cut a piece of the top fabric, allowing extra for turnings. The fabric for the back should have a loose weave, so that a blunt needle can be pushed between the threads without cutting a hole in it. Calico is suitable. Cut a piece the same size as the top and smooth them together, then baste them to prevent the layers from shifting. Mark the design on the top fabric.

2 Stitch along the marked lines by hand or machine in double channels, a scant ¼ inch apart. If sewing by hand, use a running stitch or backstitch. If sewing by machine, use a medium stitch. If the design has lines which cross each other, decide which will be a continuous line, and stop the intersecting lines of stitching at the point where they cross each other, so the cord can be threaded through.

3 Using a blunt needle with a big eye, thread a length of quilting wool into it, and working from the back, insert the needle into the stitched channel, pushing it between the loose weave of the backing fabric and the top fabric. Slide the needle along as far as possible, then bring it out farther along the channel, and pull gently to ease the wool through, leaving an end of about ¼ inch.

Reinsert the needle through the same opening and continue, leaving a small loop at the point of exit so that the wool will lie smoothly on curves and angles. At the end of the length, bring the needle out, and cut off the wool leaving ¼ inch. If the design is circular,

starting and finishing at the same point, stitch the two ends together to prevent them from disappearing into the channel.

4 Completed panel of corded quilting, using simple heart-shaped motifs.

Wholecloth quilts
Italian or corded quilting has often featured on quilts made throughout Europe, as well as in Asia and the Middle East. The wholecloth quilt illustrated above uses Italian quilting to provide intricate decoration and relief. The designs of wholecloth quilts are characteristically inspired by everyday objects, such as feathers, shells, fans, or, as in this case, flowers and leaves. The use of the same color thread for the quilting as the background fabric is also typical of wholecloth quilting, and contributes to its simple, traditional quality.

SASHIKO

Sashiko is a form of quilting which originated in Japan as a plain running stitch to strengthen or repair fabric, either padded or unpadded. The resulting fabric was put to a variety of uses, notably in firemen's clothing (which would be drenched with water before firefighting), and in clothing and household furnishings. Decorative sashiko stitching developed during the 18th century and was used for embellishing kimonos, hangings and futon covers. Designs such as "Hempweed," "Waves" and "Chrysanthemums" were inspired by nature; others were taken from family crests. The stitches are longer than a normal quilting stitch, and are done in a thread which contrasts with the cloth; black on white, or white on a blue or red ground and vice versa, are popular Japanese colors. Emphasis is not placed on the size of the stitches; it is more important that they should be even and show up well.

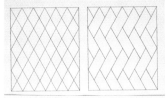

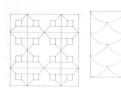

1 Start by working a square or rectangular panel of about 8 to 10 inches. A geometric design using straight lines would be a good starting project. Draw it full size on graph paper (either squared or isometric), then transfer to the fabric, using dressmaker's carbon paper.

2 Assemble the layers. For preference, use a flat, low-loft batting; too much thickness will be difficult to stitch through.

3 Begin with a knot concealed between the layers, and try as far as possible to work continuous lines of stitching, which avoids breaking the thread too often.

4 Try to achieve evenness in the stitches. The sashiko stitch is traditionally longer than stitches used for other quilting.

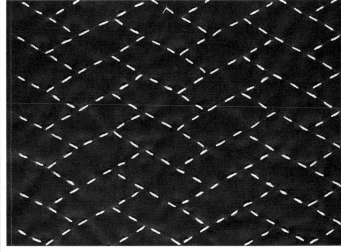

5 A thicker thread such as coton perlé no. 3, in a color that contrasts with the ground, will give a good definition.

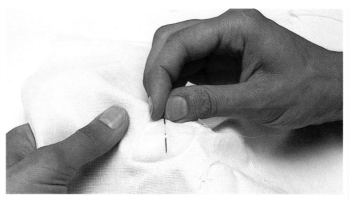

TRAPUNTO

In the technique of trapunto, the top layer of the quilt or wall hanging is lined, and selected areas are outlined with running stitch. Batting is pushed into these areas from the back to emphasize them, and make them stand out more distinctly. Trapunto can be combined successfully with other forms of quilting. It is very effective with a closely quilted background, or with linear details added in Italian quilting.

It was used to decorate clothing in the 17th and 18th centuries, and as a way of embellishing quilts, thus showing off the skills of the maker. Designs for trapunto should be made up of small areas which can be outlined individually. Fruit, foliage and flower shapes can all be simplified, and used as a basis for trapunto designs.

1 When you have worked out a satisfactory design, transfer it onto the top fabric. A pale-colored fabric with a slight glaze will show off the characteristics best, reflecting the light and emphasizing the sculptured effect. Baste the top fabric to the backing, which should be fairly soft and loosely woven. Calico or mull are both suitable fabrics.

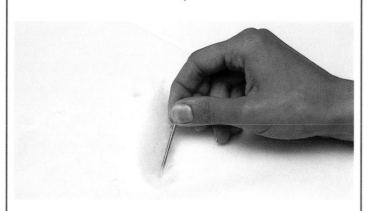

2 Stitch around each of the shapes in the design by hand, or machine using a small running stitch. Finish thread ends neatly.

Make a small slit in the back of each of the shapes, and gently insert wisps of batting,

3 When the area has enough batting pushed up to the stitching line, either stitch the gap with the edges just meeting, or rearrange the threads to close it. Do not pull

using a tool such as a knitting needle or tapestry needle with a blunt end. If the fabric has a loose enough weave, you may be able to separate the threads, and make an opening wide enough to insert batting without cutting the backing.

the stitches too tightly, as this may pucker the background. If you are combining the technique with Italian quilting, work the cording at this stage as well.

4 The piece can then be treated as a normal quilt top and assembled with the backing and batting for further quilting.

FINISHING

Once the quilt top is complete, you must decide how it is going to be quilted. Any quilt-marking lines should be made before the three layers of the quilt are assembled. The simplest form of quilting is contour-quilting which follows the shape of the patchwork pieces. More complicated quilting designs can be drawn with stencils or quilting templates. Identify the center of the quilt top and work outward. You may need to mark guidelines on the quilt top in order to position the stencils correctly.

Quilting designs are usually made up of one or more pattern elements: motifs, which form the central focus of the design and sometimes the corner details; borders, which are linear as in running feather and cables; and infill stitches, often geometric grid-type patterns.

Quilting designs form a study in themselves, with the quilting stitches performing the dual function of holding the three layers of the quilt together and decorating the surface in low relief.

Jennie Lewis,
In the Pond.
This random "Log Cabin" quilt has machine-stitched quilting and the border is made up of different colored strips of fabric.

SETTING THE BLOCKS

ASSEMBLING THE QUILT

BINDING

DISPLAYING QUILTS

MAINTAINING AND STORING QUILTS

SETTING THE BLOCKS

When you have made up enough blocks to complete the quilt top, you can stitch them together in a variety of ways.

Edge to edge, straight set
Stitch them together in the same way as the blocks are made up, right sides together, matching points and taking ¼-inch seam allowance. Press seams as you progress.

Alternate plain and patterned blocks
Pieced or appliquéd blocks can be alternated with plain ones. This will lessen the amount of work involved in the piecing or appliqué part of making the quilt. The plain blocks can be used as a showcase for more elaborate quilting designs.

Sashing
Stitch the blocks in rows with a strip of sashing between each one. Then stitch a long strip between the rows, making sure that the blocks line up across the strips. Sashing strips can be made of plain or harmonizing fabric, or they can have pieced details, such as connecting corner squares, set in a contrasting fabric.

Diagonal set
The quilt blocks can be set "on point," so that squares appear as diamonds. Stitch the blocks together in diagonal, rather than straight rows. These can be all patterned, or alternated with plain blocks in the same way as the straight set. Finish the end of each row with a triangle half the size of the finished block. Finish each corner with a triangle that is a quarter the size of the finished block.

Borders
If a border is required, there are various options. A plain border in harmonizing fabric will provide areas for extra quilting, and serves to balance and contain the patchwork. A pieced border should complement the patchwork design. Try to relate the pieces in the border to elements in the blocks used, both by size and shape. Another option is to use several borders, perhaps alternating plain with patterned, or narrow with broader widths.

Straight-cut borders
A simple solution to the border. As the edges of the quilt top may have become stretched with handling, measure the width and length of the quilt across the center from edge to edge; this will insure a more accurate fit and avoid rippling edges. Cut two straight strips to the required length and width plus seam allowances, and stitch these to the sides. Now cut two more to match the width of the patchwork plus the added width of the first two border strips, and join these to the top and bottom. Press seams as you go.

Corner squares
This is a simple but effective border. Cut two strips each for the length of the sides and top of the patchwork, to the desired width of the border plus seam allowances. Cut four squares in contrasting fabric the same size as the width of the border strips. Join two strips to the sides of the patchwork. Now add the corner squares to the short sides of the remaining strips, and stitch these along the top and bottom, making sure that the joins match.

Mitered borders
1 Cut the border strips to the desired width. The length of each strip should equal the length of the side of the patchwork, plus a generous allowance for the width of the border, which will allow for the miters. Join the borders to the patchwork, right sides together, and stop the stitching at the seam allowance in each corner. Place the quilt top right side down on a flat surface, and fold one border over the other. Draw a straight line from the inner corner at an angle of 45 degrees to the border.

2 Reverse the positions of the borders and repeat.

3 With the right sides of the borders together, line up the marked seam lines, and stitch from the inner corner to the outer corner.

4 Before trimming away excess fabric, open the corner seam, and press it to insure that it lies flat (above). The corner will align neatly at the front (below).

ASSEMBLING THE QUILT

There are several different ways in which a quilt can be assembled, some of which are illustrated on these two pages. In each case the quilt top, batting and backing need to be secured together. You should allow 3 to 4 inches extra all around on the backing fabric and batting. Smooth the three layers together on a flat surface and baste or pin with safety pins to prevent the layers from shifting while you work. It is important to keep the three layers taut as you sew to prevent buckling or creasing which could impair the final result.

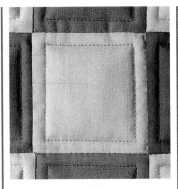

Contour-quilting
Lines of stitching are done about ⅜ inch from the seams following the outline of the patchwork shapes. Narrow masking tape can be used to mark straight lines, or you can draw them directly onto the fabric with a fabric marker.

Echo-quilting
This technique, often used in Hawaiian designs (see pages 96–97), follows the lines of appliquéd shapes. Multiple lines of stitching radiate outward to emphasize and echo the shapes.

Ditch-quilting
In this case, the stitches are worked directly onto the seam lines to define the pieced or appliquéd shapes. This is a useful technique if you don't want quilting stitches to show.

Hand-quilting
Hand-quilting can be done on your lap or the work can be fixed in a hoop or frame. Take a length of single quilting thread (about 18 inches) and run it through beeswax to strengthen it and prevent knotting. Start with a knot, and push the needle up from the back of the quilt, tugging until the knot pops through. The quilting stitch is a small, even running stitch through the three layers of the quilt. Work with one hand on top of the quilt and one underneath to guide the needle back, and to insure that each stitch has gone through all three layers. Protect both hands with a thimble on both the top stitching finger and the bottom guiding finger.

Random-quilting
Random-quilting can be worked by hand or machine. The design need not be marked as it is "drawn" freehand as you stitch. Define the area to be quilted in this manner either by the patchwork, or by drawing a shape onto the quilt top within which to stitch. Use a freeform design which covers the area evenly, and stitch by hand or machine.

Machine-quilting
This can be done either with a straight sewing stitch or by dropping the feed dogs on the machine and stitching freehand. Mark quilting lines if necessary, and prepare the quilt layers as for hand-quilting.

Knot-quilting
The quickest way to finish a quilt is to tie knots at regular intervals to secure the three layers together, rather than stitch through them. Assemble the quilt layers as for other methods, then decide at which points on the quilt to tie the knots. The patchwork design could be used as a guide. A thicker batting can be used to make a tied-quilt, giving a fluffier result. Using a strong, natural-fiber thread such as embroidery or crochet cotton, take a stitch through all three layers, leaving an end long enough to tie. Stitch again over the first stitch, bringing the needle up near the loose end. Tie in a reef knot, not too tightly as this might cause the fabric to tear. Tie at regular intervals over the quilt surface, about 4 to 6 inches apart. The knots can be used as decorative features either by themselves or in conjunction with buttons, beads or French knots.

1 For straight stitch machine-quilting, use a walking foot if possible. This feeds the three layers of the quilt through the machine evenly. Start with three or four very small stitches, then turn the stitch length to 3. Tighten the bottom tension very slightly. Quilt in the ditch between blocks to stabilize them, then follow your desired quilting design. Try to keep the bulk of the quilt rolled up and supported on a table. Use cycle clips to keep the quilt in place.

2 Try to work out a quilting design that has as few breaks as possible and avoids turning the quilt in the machine. Place your hands around the quilting area in a triangle as it goes through the machine. Thread for machine-quilting can be selected to blend or contrast with the fabrics. An invisible thread has been developed for machine-quilting. When using this thread, put ordinary machine thread which matches the quilt backing in the bobbin.

3 For free machine-quilting, change to the darning foot, drop the feed dogs, and sew by moving the work under the needle in the desired design. If possible, avoid turning it too much in the machine. Work at a steady pace, and keep the stitches a consistent size. When the feed dogs are dropped, you have to control this. Pull thread ends to the back, and cut them off close to the quilt surface.

BINDING

When quilting is completed, the raw edges of the quilt must be neatened. This can be done in various ways.

Binding can be made on the straight grain or the bias grain. Straight binding makes a more economical use of fabric, and is therefore more suitable for large quilts. Bias binding is stretchy, and is therefore good for wallhangings as it will pull in the edges slightly, and so help the quilt to hang flat against the wall.

Edges turned in
Trim away the excess batting and backing fabric so that the three layers are even. Fold the backing fabric ¼ inch over the batting, and turn in the top by ¼ inch to the wrong side. Slipstitch the folded edges of the top and backing together, completely enclosing the batting.

The completed cover of the quilt should align neatly with no puckered edges or batting visible.

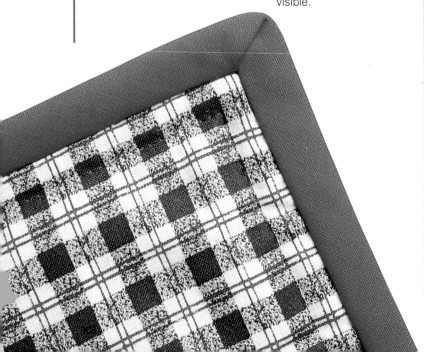

Self-binding
In this method the backing fabric is folded over the front of the quilt and hemmed down to neaten the edges. Trim the batting even with the quilt top. Mark a line 1 inch away from the edges on the backing fabric, and cut along the line. This leaves the backing extending beyond the edges by 1 inch all the way around.

Bring the backing over the front of the quilt with a double fold, enclosing the batting and raw edges. Hem down on the right side of the quilt.

At the corners, fold the backing so that the point touches the corner point of the quilt top, and trim away excess fabric along the crease. Then fold the ends under to form a miter (see page 105), and continue hemming the backing over the front of the quilt.

Making the binding

A double binding is easier to handle, and gives a neater and stronger finish.

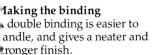

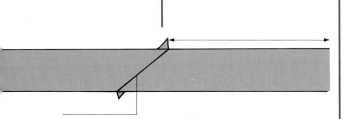

Straight binding

Cut strips on the straight grain of the fabric from selvedge to selvedge 2 to 2½ inches wide.

If it is necessary to join strips, a join on an angle is less noticeable.

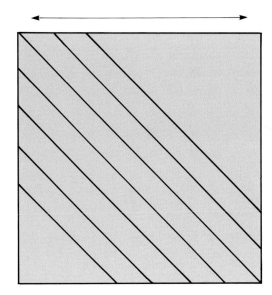

Bias binding

Cut the strips diagonally across a square of fabric. One square yard will make about 17½ yards of 2-inch-wide bias tape.

2 To join pieces, place the straight grain ends, right sides together, and stitch, taking ¼-inch seam allowance.

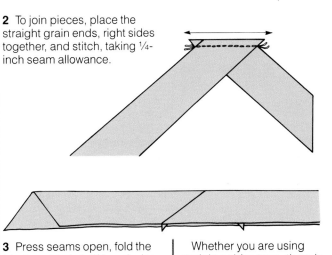

3 Press seams open, fold the binding strip in half lengthwise and press. Trim away seam allowance ends.

Whether you are using straight or bias tape, there is now one side with two raw edges and one side with a fold.

Applying binding

To apply binding, begin in the center of one side of the quilt, and place the raw edges against the edges to be bound. Stitch through both layers of the binding and through all layers of the quilt, taking ¼-inch seam allowance. The folded edges of the binding can then be turned over the raw edges of the quilt, and hemmed down on the back of the quilt.

DISPLAYING QUILTS

Although quilts were made originally to be displayed on the horizontal plane of a bed or table, their decorative qualities were always considered by the maker and admired by the viewer. As early as in the 19th century, quilts were displayed as hangings in shows and competitions, albeit temporarily. By the 1920s quilts were becoming collectible, and the combination of their visual and tactile qualities made them an appealing addition to interior decoration. Today, more quilts than ever before are being made for vertical display as wallhangings.

A newly completed quilt should be signed and dated by the maker. Embroider the relevant details directly onto the back of your quilt or onto a label which can be stitched to the back. Indelible pens with which you can write straight onto fabric are also available.

To display a quilt as a wallhanging, either sew a continuous casing along the top through which a hanging rod can be inserted, or use Velcro tape. Whichever method you use, cut the wood marginally shorter than the width of the quilt, so it will be concealed when the quilt is hung. Choose a hanging position out of direct sunlight to preserve the colors in the fabrics, and be aware of other atmospheric conditions that may damage a quilt; smoke and dampness should be avoided. A quilt should not be hung indefinitely, it is a good idea to "rest" textiles for a short period after six months or so.

Making a hanging sleeve
Measure the width of the quilt and cut a piece of fabric this length and 8 to 10 inches wide. Fold in half lengthwise with right sides together, and stitch into a long tube; turn right side out. Turn a narrow hem to the inside at each end, leaving the ends open. Slip-hem the casing tube along its two long edges across the top of the quilt. A batten or rod, which does not touch the back of the quilt, can be inserted through the casing and suspended at each end. For a very heavy quilt, make the casing in two sections so that the quilt can be supported in the center by a third hanger. Turn under a narrow hem at each end of each section of casing before hemming the two tubes to the back of the quilt, leaving a gap in the center to expose the rod.

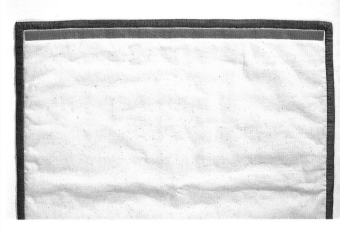

Using Velcro tape
Cut a length of 2-inch-wide Velcro slightly shorter than the width of the quilt top. Machine-stitch one side of the Velcro to a length of cotton tape, then hand-stitch this to the reverse side of the quilt along the top. Stitch through the backing and batting so that the quilt will be adequately supported, but make sure that no stitches show on the front of the quilt. The other side of the Velcro is then glued to a length of wood which can be fixed in place where the quilt is to hang. To attach the quilt to it, apply even pressure so that the quilt will be adequately supported.

MAINTAINING AND STORING QUILTS

The time, skill and materials invested in the making of any quilt deserve consideration in its treatment and care. It is sensible to try and preserve it, therefore, whether its value is primarily as a part of family history or whether it is a contemporary quilt to be enjoyed both now and in the future.

If you have an old quilt which needs cleaning, remember it may be fragile and must be cleaned with this in mind. A museum in your area may have a textile conservator who would advise you on the composition of the fabrics and batting and suitable cleaning methods. Silk and wool should always be dry-cleaned; seek a quality dry cleaner with a good reputation; the wardrobe department of a theater may be able to advise.

Cotton and linen could be washed if the fabrics are not too damaged. First remove loose dust by spreading the quilt on a flat surface, covering it with calico and vacuuming it on a gentle setting. Test fabrics for dyefastness by pressing dampened white blotting paper against them. Wash the quilt by hand in the bathtub, agitating gently in several changes of water. Use a mild detergent; gentle ones are now available for delicate fabrics. Use the

shower spray to rinse out any remaining cleaner. Squeeze out as much excess water as possible by hand. To dry the quilt, place it flat on layers of absorbent material such as towels. Do not strain old fabrics and delicate stitching with the weight of the remaining water by hanging them. New quilts can be machine-washed on the gentle setting of the washing machine, using a mild, color-care detergent. If all fabrics have been prewashed before the quilt was made, there should be no problem with colors running. All fabrics, whether new or old, should be protected from direct sunlight to avoid fading the colors and damaging any of the fibers.

Quilt storage

Anyone with knowledge of textile conservation will tell you that correct storage is an important factor in preserving and extending the life of all fabrics. Whether you are storing old or new quilts, the following points are applicable. Try if possible to store quilts flat; on a bed is the ideal place. If this is not practical, roll the quilt around a long, cardboard tube which has been covered with acid-free tissue paper, using tissue to separate the layers as well. If folding is the only storage method possible due to shortage of space, refold every two or three months to prevent the fabrics from wearing at the creases, and pack the layers with acid-free tissue paper. Wrap quilts, whether rolled or folded, in white cotton sheeting, never plastic, and store in a dry atmosphere. Dampness causes mildew which will permanently mark fabrics. Make sure that quilts are clean before putting them into storage, as the fibers can also be damaged by dust and grime. Shake gently to remove any dust and use the vacuum cleaner as previously described if washing or dry cleaning is not possible. Quilts which have survived from previous generations are our legacy to enjoy and preserve. Similarly, those quilts being made today will become the family heirlooms of tomorrow.

Jenny Rees,
Fan Quilt.
Proper maintenance will ensure colors never fade, and will preserve the quilt for future generations.

Peter, Peter,
pumpkin-eater...

THEMES

THE VERSATILITY OF QUILTMAKING AS A MEANS OF CREATIVE EXPRESSION HAS BEEN INCREASINGLY RECOGNIZED BY NEEDLEWORKERS AT EVERY LEVEL OF ABILITY. TO INTERPRET OR REPRODUCE THE TRADITIONAL PATTERNS GIVES MANY PEOPLE THE SATISFACTION OF MAKING SOMETHING BOTH USEFUL AND BEAUTIFUL. ALTERNATIVELY, THE TECHNIQUES INVOLVED PROVIDE A BASIS FOR EXPERIMENTATION, LEADING TO UNIQUELY INDIVIDUAL WORKS. HISTORICAL REASONS FOR MAKING QUILTS HAVE ALWAYS BEEN DIVERSE, RANGING FROM ECONOMIC NECESSITY TO THE EXHIBITION OF ELABORATE NEEDLEWORK AND EXPENSIVE FABRICS. THE TIME AND SKILL EXPENDED ON HISTORICAL QUILTS ARE APPARENT IN THE ARTISTRY OF CONTEMPORARY QUILTMAKERS, ILLUSTRATING THE ENDURING ATTRACTION OF THIS IMAGINATIVE CRAFT.

Fairfield Processing Corp.
group quilt
Once Upon a Nursery Rhyme
65 × 80 inches

TRADITIONS

HISTORICAL QUILTS

Traditional quilt designs are those that have been passed on through generations of quiltmakers reflecting the basic principles of quilt design. These traditions are defined by techniques, those of patchwork, appliqué and quilting being the basics from which others grew.

There are many forms within these traditions. Block quilts can be simple, as in the nine-patch square, or more elaborate, using smaller and more complicated shapes or curved seams in patterns such as "Double Wedding Ring," or "New York Beauty" to show off your skills. Medallion quilts, with a large central motif enclosed in a series of borders, test the design skills of the quiltmaker, and can combine the two techniques of appliqué and patchwork. The wholecloth quilt, another traditional form, exploits the texture that close stitching through the three layers of a quilt creates with highly intricate designs stitched on plain fabric. There are many different traditions in wholecloth quilting, and these are particularly strong in North America, the North of England, and Wales. This kind of quilting was often done in groups at a quilting bee.

Many quilt historians make the link between quiltmaking and a more diverse social history of women, drawing references from documented examples in contemporary diaries and letters. A patchwork quilt containing scraps of fabric from family clothing and household furnishings was often the only link with home for a young bride living far from her loved ones. Needlework was seen as a necessary accomplishment for all girls, and quiltmaking was often taught from an early age to develop these skills. A first quilt may have been simple squares such as in a checkerboard design, leading to more elaborate block designs as skills increased. Even within these confines, the personal expression of an individual can always be detected. Choice of fabrics, block, set and quilting designs make for infinite possibilities. Sometimes patterns were modified, so they never became static but continued to develop as a living heritage. As you study the quilts in this section, you will be aware of the personality of the makers stamped on the quilts. In history, as in the present, quilters were guided but never confined by these continuing traditions.

Fairfield Processing Corp. group quilt,
American Heritage Quilt.
65 × 80 inches

This "American Heritage" quilt uses a variety of techniques to celebrate its themes. Key events in the history of the United States of America are presented within a patriotic framework which uses elements of the Stars and Stripes to link the separate blocks. These are made in a combination of techniques which include patchwork, appliqué and quilting. Further details are added to the quilt with embroidery.

Klara Atalla,
Challenge 2.
31 × 31 inches

A machine-pieced and hand-quilted crazy quilt which uses the "center piece" method. That is, random shapes are added to a center piece to make the individual blocks. The distinct color changes between the main part of the quilt and the border make a pleasing contrast between the two areas.

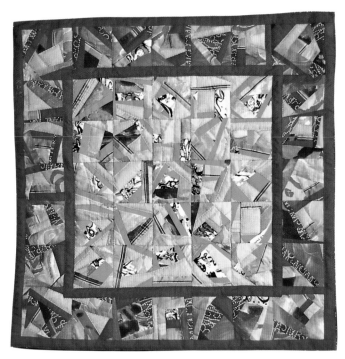

Katharine Guerrier,
og Cabin, Courthouse Steps.
4 × 14 inches

he "Courthouse Steps" log abin block is just one variation f this versatile design. Dark nd light value fabrics are placed opposite each other in the block. When these are used in multiples, a design reminiscent of Chinese lanterns emerges. A narrow, stripped border contains the quilt blocks, emphasizing the linear qualities of the pattern.

Ingrid Wieland,
Delfter Impression.
47 × 33 inches

This appliqué basket quilt has the naive charm of much folk art. A central medallion with its flower bouquet made of many blue fabrics, some of which use three-dimensional effects, is framed by a narrow blue octagon on a cream ground. Border details of repeating flower heads and leaf swags finish the composition. The combination of cream and blue gives this quilt the delicate appeal of Delft china.

▶ **Polly Mitchell,**
Sophie's Quilt.
74 × 74 inches

Amish-style basket blocks in a typical range of colors form the center of this quilt. They are surrounded by a red border with pink corner squares. Broad outer borders provide plain areas for hand-quilted running cable designs. A mix of cultures is represented in this quilt; to quote the maker, "Sophie wanted an Amish design and was studying in China at the time, so the quilting patterns were inspired by Chinese symbols and decoration."

▲ **Suzon de Marcilly,**
L'étoile de Marinière.
95 × 95 inches

Composed of elements from the "Mariner's Compass" and "Broken Star" designs, this is a challenge for the ambitious quiltmaker. The example shown here displays a sensitive choice of colors in earth tones enlivened by flashes of yellow. The large star is set on a cream ground and contained by a double border with corner details reflected from the central design.

▲ **Daphne Ramsey,**
Cathedral Window Wall Hanging.
30 × 30 inches

This variation on the "Cathedral Window" technique distorts the regular pattern, elongating some of the "petal" shapes. Machine-embroidered crazy patchwork in the spaces frame the center diamond and add further interest. This piece was inspired by the modern stained-glass rose window in Coventry Cathedral, England. Silk and calico are used with both hand- and machine-techniques. A narrow, mitered border finishes the edges of the quilt.

Nancy Breland,
First Light.
52 × 67 inches

An extensive collection of blue and cream fabrics are displayed in this elegant quilt. Skillful handling of color values gives an impressionistic view of the dawn rising slowly upward toward the stars, still shining in the night sky. Their sharp points, together with the circular secondary designs (detail, left), convey a dynamic energy. The quilt is machine-pieced and hand-quilted.

Katharine Guerrier,
Rail Fence Miniature.
13½ × 14 inches

Quick machine-strip piecing was used in this miniature quilt, made to preserve and showcase old fabrics purchased on a trip to America. The "bubblegum pink" fabric is typical of fabrics produced in the 1930s depression era. The yellow is also of the same period – others are made to resemble old fabrics, packaged as "instant antiques," reflecting the current interest in nostalgia. The block is an extremely simple one composed of four rectangles. The quilt has a double border, each set with corner squares, and is finished with a narrow maroon binding. It is machine-quilted with invisible thread.

▶ **Gill Turley,**
Fabric of Oxfam.
54 × 76 inches

This rather striking quilt was made entirely from recycled shirting fabrics purchased in charity Oxfam shops. A cross-shaped central medallion is set in a grid of geometric shapes in a muted, monochromatic color scheme which is pleasingly somber. The patches were rotary-cut and machine-pieced, and the quilt is finished with a double bias-binding and tie-quilting.

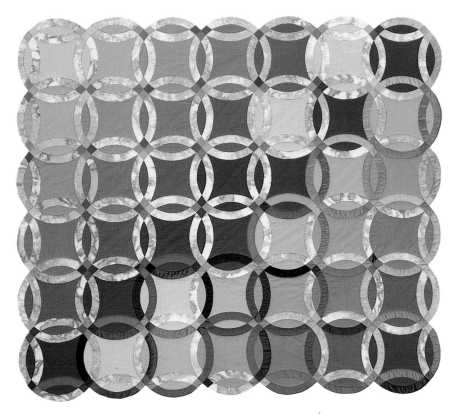

◀ **Grania McElliot,**
Fractured Wedding Rings.
68 × 78 inches

A skillful interpretation of this difficult design in a variety of subtle colors, ranging from cream through mauve and dark blues/purples with accents of burgundy. The shape of the block extends into the border, an effect that gives the quilt a feeling of lightness. This quilt is machine-pieced using cotton and silk fabrics as contrasts, and incorporates some hand-dyed cottons as well. It is machine-quilted.

◀ **Gill Turley,**
Wild Rose.
40 × 40 inches

A wholecloth quilt with a center diamond medallion containing Celtic and fan motifs with a fine, feather border. A straight filling

pattern and more fans separate the outer border from the center square, which is composed of flowing, floral scrolls (detail below). The effect created by the stitching in this composition of traditional quilting designs is that of a bas-relief carving.

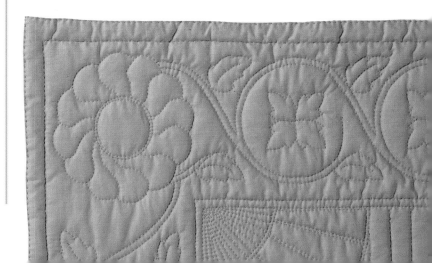

▶ **Rita Ball,**
Recyclomat.
52 × 72 inches

Inspired by Australian "Wagga Wagga" quilts, which were made from clothing tacked to a foundation, often an old blanket, and made to be strictly functional in the face of shortage and hardship, this quilt comments on the origins of quiltmaking as a means of recycling fabric into bedding. All the clothing is flattened and stitched with embroidery yarn to the backing using blanket stitch. In addition to being a usable bed cover, the quilt has a built-in "activity" aspect – the buttons and zippers open to reveal picture T-shirts and the pockets can still be used. Made for an exhibition with the theme "Oxfam, working for a fairer world," this quilt was perhaps intended to point out the inequality of living conditions in rich and poor countries.

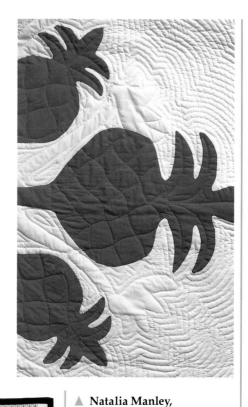

Natalia Manley,
Olivier's Quilt.
117 × 125 inches

The traditional "Pineapple" motif (detail of back, above far right) is combined with that of birds-of-paradise in this Hawaiian appliqué quilt. It is reversible, with a simplified version of the appliqué on the back. Completed in the traditional style of quilting, which echoes the central appliqué or "Kapa Lau," this is a fine example of the form.

Gill Turley,
tars of The North.
4 × 44 inches

his quilt is a variation of the Log Cabin" block; by altering ne width of the strips between ne light and dark sides of each lock, an illusion of curved lines achieved. Skillfully handled olor values in a restricted alette of grays add to the lusion by making the dark tars seem to float in front of the ghter diamond shapes behind nem. The quilt is machine-ieced and hand-quilted, and nished with a double binding.

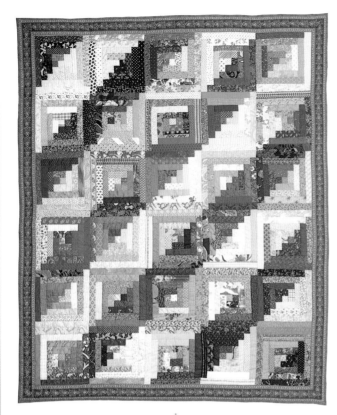

▲ Gillian Newberry,
Charm Quilt.
86 × 86 inches

The "Log Cabin" design is an all-time favorite and ideal for making scrap quilts. This example, set in the "Straight Furrow" variation, is also a charm quilt, that is, no fabric is used more than once. Different-scale printed fabrics enliven the quilt surface, making points of interest to hold the eye. The quilt is nicely framed with a narrow border fabric. It is machine-pieced and hand-quilted.

▼ Jenni Dobson,
Winter's Joy.
63 × 44 inches

Circular Japanese-inspired "Marumon" blocks are hand-appliquéd, then scattered and hand-stitched to the peach-colored background. Most of the blocks feature some hand-embroidery. The background is hand-quilted in a traditional Japanese design called "Sayagata." The outer border is turned to the back and hand-sewn in place.

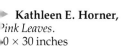
Kathleen E. Horner,
Pink Leaves.
30 × 30 inches

The pink leaves are hand-
appliquéd, some being first
embellished with machine-
embroidery. The stems are
made from a 1-inch bias strip,
and are also hand-appliquéd.
The contour quilting is done "by
eye," not marked. A narrow
binding finishes the edge.

◀ **Frederike Kohlhaussen,**
Snail Trail.
53 × 53 inches

A symmetrical arrangement of
this intriguing traditional
pattern, the contrast is between
colored and black fabrics. The
effect is of curves, but only
straight seams are used. The
coloring in the corner blocks
provides a different focus,
further underlining the illusion.
The quilt is machine-pieced
and hand-quilted.

▶ **Jo Walters/Ernestine Dearwent,**
But Soft.
44 × 56 inches

Machine-pieced "Bowtie" blocks in an octagonal set, many of which feature hand-dyed fabrics, give this quilt a luminous quality. The regularity of the blocks is offset by the subtle color variations within the fabrics. A narrow inner border separates the blocks from the outer border of pieced strips, ranging through the colors from dark through to light.

▶ **Nancy Breland,**
Mosaic.
75 × 58 inches

The complex geometry of this quilt rewards sustained study for the many secondary designs that become apparent. Made as "an experiment in using yellow," it contains many different fabrics organized into a coherent, complete design. Machine-pieced and hand-quilted.

◄ **Kathleen E. Horner,**
Strippy Quilt – Flying Geese,
Blue Daisy.
77 × 98 inches

The strippy quilt is a traditional form typical of the Northeast of England. This example is machine-pieced using the quick piecing rotary-cut method. The quilting pattern (detail above) was devised to complement the straight lines. Large daisy shapes were drawn onto the quilt top using a handmade template, and the rest of the quilting designs were added freehand using an artist's colored pencil. The quilting was stitched by hand in a large frame and the edges turned in and hemmed together.

► **Katharine Guerrier,**
Broken Dishes Miniature.
15 × 15 inches

Deceptively simple, this quilt is made from a combination of plain and pieced blocks. The quick machine-pieced "Broken Dishes" is made up of only eight triangles but, by alternating these with plain squares and placing them in the diamond set illustrated and with a center star, a more sophisticated design emerges. The printed fabric is Javanese batik. The quilt is machine-pieced and machine-quilted.

▶ **Gene Bowen,**
Amish Center Diamond.
76 × 76 inches

A traditional Amish-inspired quilt of classic simplicity. The center diamond is bordered in gray with corner squares, and set in a red ground. Further borders add to the overall design and provide areas for some of the traditional quilting motifs of the Amish: flowers, vines and baskets.

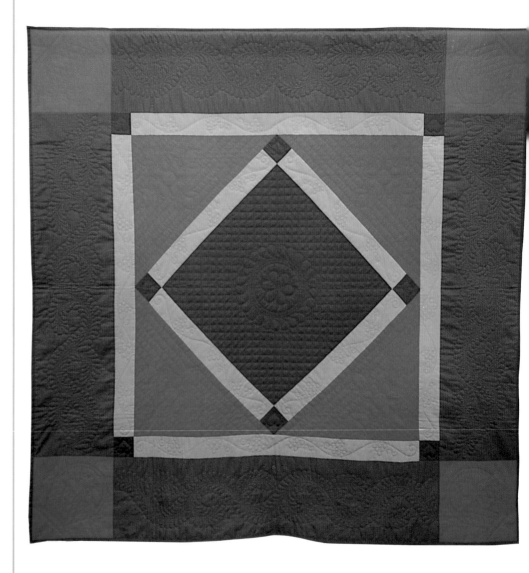

◀ **Katharine Guerrier,**
Log Cabin, Straight Furrow.
14 × 11½ inches

In this small log cabin quilt the blocks are set together in the "Straight Furrow" design in which the dark and light areas form strong diagonal lines.

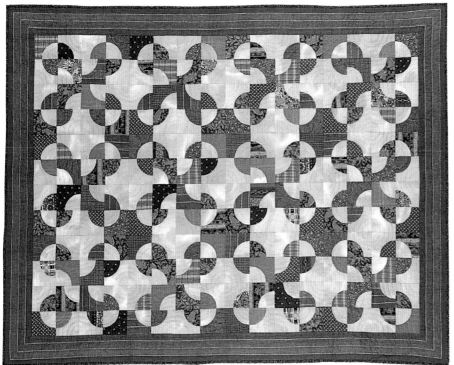

◀ **Jo Walters,**
"I am a Friend of Bill W."
Drunkard's Path Variation.
44 × 56 inches

This simple block with a curved seam, ideal for a scrap quilt, joins a dark piece and a light piece together. The blocks can then be set in a variety of different designs according to the direction in which the dark/light lines are placed. In this version the darks and lights are reversed alternately, which serves to produce a complex secondary design. Machine-pieced and hand-quilted.

NEW EXPRESSIONS

CONTEMPORARY QUILTS

New movements in any art form are often subject to scrutiny and criticism by the purists, but this does not stop artists from exploring fresh avenues, developing techniques and using their chosen medium to make personal statements. So it is in the world of quiltmaking, where many artists are now choosing fabric and stitching as their preferred medium. Quilts are no longer thought of as purely functional, and many quiltmakers are producing work specifically intended for display. The quilt is now accepted as a craft-based contemporary art worthy of attention just as "fine" art is, and subject to the same critical appraisal. These quilters, rather than just reproducing traditional quilt patterns, draw on the same wide range of sources for their inspirations as artists working in other media. This is not to say that the traditions in quiltmaking are completely disregarded but rather that they are expanded and interpreted by many contemporary quilt artists. Personal observation based on drawing

or photography is used as the inspiration for the quilt by Kate Wells, *Anemone Quilt*. Others find inspiration in a specific message or question, such as *Struggle for Hope* by Claudine Joho or *Where Has All The Magic Gone* by Rita Scannell. The textures and colors in the fabrics themselves or even the techniques employed may also be a starting point, as in *Pictures in the Fire* by Carole Proctor. The formalized structure of certain contemporary quilts may be integral to their meaning, as in the work of Michael James or Bridget Ingram Bartholomaus, whilst the combination of curved shapes and vivid colors is exploited by Irena Goos in *Flying School* to evoke a dramatic sense of movement. The revival of interest in quiltmaking that began in the early 1960s and 1970s has led to its recognition as a dynamic art form.

Whatever the initial source of inspiration, these quilts represent a new and exciting collection by artists keen to express their ideas and beliefs in fabric and stitching.

Michael James,
Processional.
× 118 inches

Michael James has a distinguished career as a quiltmaker, being one of the foremost American practitioners of the craft. In commenting on *Processional*, one of a group of five quilts made in 1992, he is quoted as saying, "In *Processional* the intent was to reflect a series of highly formalized movements, such as those that might define traditional Japanese dance or pantomime. Each visual gesture here is dependent on the sequences of tensions and forces that exist among the bracketing and bracketed figures."

 Bethan Ash,
amp Art 3.
× 95 inches

"trip" and "Seminole" techniques are used in this vibrant quilt, inspired at first by the silk fabric. The maker says, "I really wanted a quilt which would shout, 'Look at me, I want to be noticed'!" More, and similar, fabrics were collected and the desired effect was achieved. Machine-pieced and machine-quilted.

◀ **Irena Goos,**
Meeting.
40 × 51 inches

"A fascination with space, light and movement" inspired this quilt. These concepts are expressed with a powerful three-dimensional effect created by the manipulation of color, tonal value and shape. The quilt is machine-pieced with straight and curved seams, and machine-quilted.

Katharine Guerrier,
Crazy Stars 1 and *Crazy Stars 2*
Both quilts measure 60 × 60
inches

These two quilts form part of a
series in the exploration of colour
values in dark, medium and
light. *Crazy Stars 1* is
composed of dark/light
diamond-shaped blocks,
divided into contained crazy
shapes and linked by stars
which are visible because they
contrast with the values in the
main body of each block.
Corner blocks composed of
dark shapes with light "floats"
define the large diamond.
Crazy Stars 2 uses three colour
values. The blocks are
composed of medium/dark
values, while the light ones are
reserved for the stars, which
makes them more noticeable.
The same contained crazy
block design is used, but
values are reversed. Both quilts
are machine-pieced and
machine-quilted, and each of
them uses many hand-block-
printed and batik fabrics.

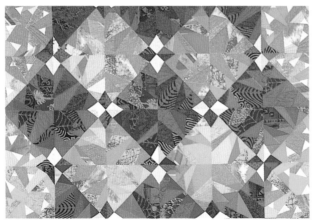

Rita Scannell,
Where Has All The Magic Gone.
36 × 54 inches

A machine-appliquéd, pieced and embroidered quilt which was "made to tell a story in abstract form using a secret, private language." Jewel-like embroidered squares are scattered on a richly textured background made of mixed media – textiles and fiberglass. Intrigued though the viewer may be by the obscure title, the composition and surface of this piece provide enough interest without the need for elaboration.

Heidrun Rinner,
Mosaik.
39 × 39 inches

A desire to combine patchwork and fabric-dyeing led to the creation of this quilt. The technique used – machine crazy patchwork – is described by the maker: "I started with a piece of fabric in the center and worked around clockwise as you go. I continued until a square was filled, then I placed the squares in an arrangement of my choice and set the blocks together." Machine-pieced and hand-quilted.

▼ **Carole Proctor,**
Pictures in the Fire.
36 × 44 inches

"An exploration of red fabrics" was the starting point for this quilt, made with rotary-cut machine-pieced strips. The whole image has an Art Deco feel to it which is perfectly complemented by the curved quilting lines done both by hand and machine.

▲ **Grania McElliot,**
Refracted Pathway.
48 × 54 inches

Made for an exhibition of kimonos, this opulent piece uses a combination of fabrics.

Silk, satin, taffeta and suede provide a rich mix of color and texture. Crazy shapes are machine-pieced for both the outside and the lining. The kimono is machine-quilted "in the ditch."

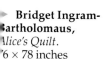 **Bridget Ingram-Bartholomaus,**
Alice's Quilt.
76 × 78 inches

The medallion set of the quilt is an effective foil for the "Seminole" strip-pieced borders, each complementing and enhancing the other in this pleasing quilt. Worked entirely by machine, including both the quilting and the embroidery.

◀ **Irena Goos,**
Flying School.
44 × 45 inches

The colors and curved shapes in this quilt combine to convey graceful movement in an attempt by the maker to depict "the flight of a bird portrayed by the repetition and movement of a flat element." The quilt is machine-pieced and machine quilted "in the ditch."

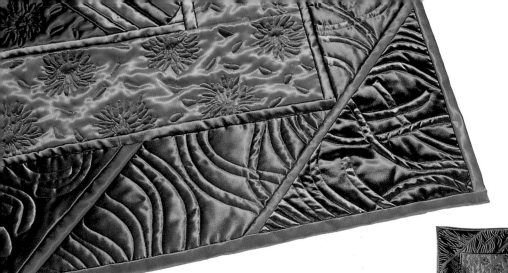

▲ Kate Wells,
Anemone Quilt.
102 × 102 inches

The inspiration for this quilt came from the vibrant colors of anemones with black stamens, their stems seen distorted through a glass vase. It is made using an adaptation of strip-patchwork, and embellished with machine-embroidery. Other details are hand-painted with acrylic fabric paints. The fabric used, a shiny slipper satin, is an ideal medium to portray the glowing colors of the flowers.

◀ Rita Scannell,
Bird of Paradise.
32 × 32 inches

An original block design constructed in the "Log Cabin" method. Note how the four-block panel creates a diamond-shaped secondary design. Spiky shapes and hot colors in silk fabrics are expressive of the exotic essence of the subject. It is machine-pieced and machine-quilted.

▲ **Katharine Guerrier,**
Abstractions.
28 × 28 inches

The same machine-pieced block is repeated nine times, and although colors and fabrics recur throughout the quilt, they are used in different positions in every block, making each one seem very different. Blocks are also turned about to alter their appearance even more. This is an exercise in balance – of shape, color and texture. Solid colors frame the blocks and the machine-quilting zigzags across the quilt to reflect the angularity of the composition.

▲ **Claudine Joho,**
Struggle For Hope.
47 × 45 inches

"There is always hope for people who open their minds and hearts." The maker of this quilt delivers a heartening personal message in a semi-abstract form. Techniques used include appliqué with machine-embroidery and machine-quilting.

Pam de Rivaz,
Rose Panel.
0 × 18 inches

This quilt makes effective use
of the "Cathedral Window" and
"Folded Star" techniques.
Delicate pink and green fabrics
in polished cotton and silk
reflect the colors of roses.

▼ **Rita Scannell,**
The Dreamer and The Dream.
36 × 53 inches

In this mystical, semi-figurative
image the maker has managed
to convey the floating,
weightless quality of dreams.
Effective use has been made of
the fabrics, which include silk
voile hand-dyed in close color
ranges and organza. All
stitching – the piecing,
appliqué and quilting – is by
machine throughout.

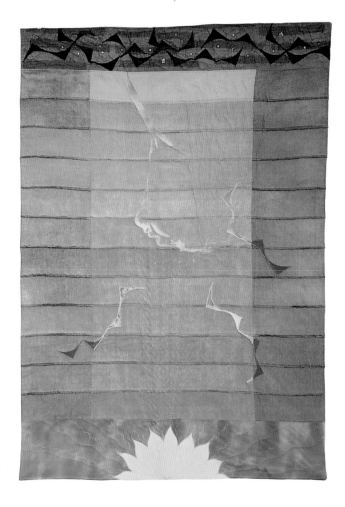

PATTERN AND RHYTHM

QUILTING DESIGNS

There is always something appealing about a series of repeated shapes, whether they are natural or man-made; flower petals, the formation of crystals or the spiral pattern in an ammonite, wrought-iron work, roof tiles or a contemporary city skyline. As we regard our environment, our eyes will investigate and attempt to collate these similar elements, arranging and rearranging them in a satisfactory way in which order and balance are achieved.

In many cultures and through the ages, the principles of pattern-making, the use of repeated shapes and geometric forms, has been recognized and exploited for its ornamental aspects. Decorative artists and craftsmen have drawn on this important source of inspiration to embellish their environ-

ment. Similar patterns occur in the mosaics of the Ancient Greeks and in the floor tiles of Renaissance Italy. Parallels can be drawn between the decorative elements in Early English stone tracery and those of the elaborate wrought-iron work of the Victorian era, and the geometric tile designs of the Alhambra in Spain can be compared with many quilts.

In this section quilts that seem to explore and extend the qualities inherent i repeated patterns have bee selected. Straightforward repet tion in the *Pineapple Log Cab* quilt by Katharine Guerrier revea secondary designs unimagine when the block is viewed as single unit. Louise Mabbs uses more sophisticated approach wit the introduction of color change across her quilts, *Taking the Libert with Rainbows* and *Origami Winds*.

Stained Glass Window by Jenni Lewis is designed to hang in window and thus make use of varied external light source to com plement the color in its panels. I her quilt, *Light and Shadow*, Frede ike Kohlhaussen seeks to represen the shifting, fragmented image formed when sun shines throug glass, by the imposition of stru tural variation upon a regula geometric block. Complex use of color and forma structure may also be given tactile impact by th addition of diagonal bugle beads, as Ann Fahl did i her work, *Triangles and Beads*. From examples in thi section, it can be seen how pattern-making can be straightforward repetition of simple shapes, or mor complex investigations involving color change within a chosen grid.

◀ **Judith Gait**
Royal Star Block (detail)

Simple shapes combined with a restricted color scheme prove that a design need not be intricate to be effective.

▲ **Jennie Lewis,**
Stained Glass Window.
35 × 35 inches

A circular stained glass window inspired this quilt made in reverse appliqué, with hand-painted silk polyester panels. It was designed to be hung in a window so that the light would shine through and illuminate the panels.

▲ **Louise Mabbs,**
Origami Winds.
30 × 30 inches

Made for an exhibition with the theme "Wind," a toy pinwheel made from folded paper provided the idea which inspired this quilt. Double-sided two-colored fabric squares are folded and sewn, sometimes with extra padding. A sequin secures the points of the squares with a stitch. A border of triangles in the same bright colors as those used in the center and contrasted with black completes this light-hearted piece. Machine- and hand-stitched.

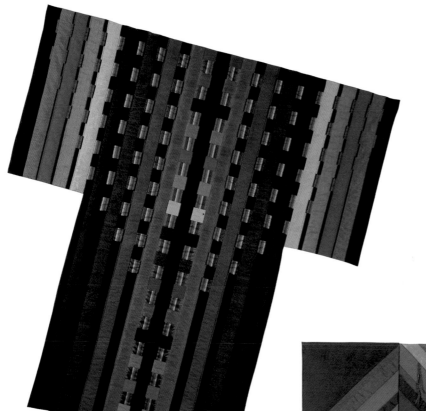

◀ **Grania McElliot,**
Fire Opal Kimono.
70 × 72 inches

A kimono-shaped wallhanging using striped and plain colored silks. The striped fabrics are contained by a lattice of plain, bright colors symmetrically arranged. The piece was made "as a color exercise" and amply demonstrates the evident delight the maker has in these vibrant colors. Machine-pieced and -quilted.

Grania McElliot,
methyst.
8 × 48 inches

nother kimono-shaped
anging in the same series.
his one is strip-pieced using
otton, silk and satin. Machine-
eced and -quilted.

◀ **Frederike Kohlhaussen,**
Light and Shadow.
62 × 56 inches

A simple, regular geometric block is changed by divisions creating interesting variations in the structure of the quilt. The design was inspired by sun shining through a window and the fragmentation of images thus created. Machine-pieced and hand-quilted.

▶ **Louise Mabbs,**
Taking The Liberty With Rainbows.
90 × 98 inches

A quilt seeking to explore three-dimensional effects. This quilt uses a wide spectrum of colors for the framework and a collection of geometric Liberty prints, hence its title. Machine-pieced and hand-quilted.

◀ Ingrid Wieland,
Monogramme.
36 × 36 inches

With a combination of the maker's monogram and a design inspired by the artist Victor Vasarely, this quilt achieves a fine balance between the colors and shapes used. Although these are essentially simple, interest is maintained through use of the different-sized circles that serve to give the quilt a sense of movement.

Isabel Schneider,
rt Deco.
2 × 42 inches

he work of artist Sonia elaunay was the starting point or this quilt, which features a lock with curved seams. This repeated nine times, with ach version made up in a ifferent combination of clear, lain colors to break the ormality of the repetition. The se of black sashing and orders separates the blocks, aking each seem like a small ork of art. Pieced by hand, nd machine- and hand-uilted.

Shelly Burge,
Chimera.
50 × 58 inches

An ingenious use of strip-piecing is demonstrated in this contemporary quilt. It is made of equilateral triangles, with those for the star blocks first strip-pieced before they are cut out. These form a broken hexagon in a field of blue triangles, and effective use is made of blue's complementary color orange. A border of angled strips is separated from the center of the quilt by a dark frame. The quilting design of overlapping rings was inspired by the ripples of the surface of a pond.

Ann Fahl,
Triangles and Beads.
61 × 47 inches

A one-patch quilt composed of triangles, but with a complexity added by the controlled use of color. Glowing red and turquoise areas are offset by the use of deep, rich colors which blend together in a multi-fabric composition. Bugle beads, sewn on in a diagonal geometric design, and machine-quilting emphasize the formal geometry of the quilt.

▲ **Catherine Schneider-Moynot,**
*Et la Lumière Fut/Disappearing
Light.*
42 × 42 inches

This interpretation of the theme
"Disappearing Light" uses a
complex repetition of controlled
crazy blocks. These interact
together to form a fragmented
whole. The expert handling of
color across the surface of the
quilt adds much to the
impression. It is machine-
pieced and hand-quilted using
hand-dyed silk.

▲ **Grania McElliot,**
Log Cabin Quilt.
104 × 104 inches

The "Log Cabin" quilt is an all-time favorite and this is a fine interpretation of the design. The blocks, set on point, are made in a limited color palette of blues, pinks and grays in varying values that clearly illustrate the versatility of this traditional block. Machine-pieced and -quilted.

Katharine Guerrier,
Pineapple Log Cabin Miniature.
13 × 11 inches

The strong contrast between
dark and light emphasizes
secondary designs when the
blocks are placed together.
Machine-pieced and -quilted.

Katharine Guerrier,
Indiana Puzzle Miniature.
15 × 15 inches

Positive and negative
interlocking shapes are created
as these simple blocks
composed only of squares and
triangles are put together. The
secret is in the placement of
dark and light values within the
block. A simple stripped border
is separated from the center
of the quilt by a narrow,
dark band.

TEXTURE

THE QUILT SURFACE

When asked why they prefer the medium of fabric and stitching over others, many quilt artists say that the texture of the fabric and stitching gives a unique quality to the quilts; a tactile surface unlike that in any other media. This, combined with the visual appeal of the surface pattern on a quilt, allows the maker another dimension to explore when working with fabrics.

A textured surface can be achieved in a variety of ways. Reflective and matt-textured fabrics can be juxtaposed to contrast their individual qualities, as in Mrs A. Small's *Egyptian Necklace*. Surface stitchery may also be used to enhance the qualities inherent in the fabrics. In *Splitter/Splinter*, for example, Klara Atalla contrasts the pattern of fine seams with the directional weave of the base fabric, silk.

The visual texture on printed fabrics is exploited effectively by Louise Mabbs in *African King Violet*. In this quilt, a combination of batik fabrics in blues and yellows is complemented by solid areas in the same color range.

The clever manipulation of different textures may also be used to produce the illusion of solidity or movement within the pattern of a quilt. *Fabric Roll* by Mary Fogg creates an illusion of a three-dimensional image by its skillful incorporation of strips of cotton and silk. *Liberty Belle* blends the different prints of various fabrics to give an impression of movement to the design's straight lines.

Close-quilting was originally done to prevent the raw wool or cotton filler in the quilt from bunching together at one end, but its potential as an added textural feature was realized and exploited in the elaborately stitched designs on old quilts. Other ways of achieving special effects with fabric that can be incorporated into quilts are outlined in the pages on techniques: experimentation may lead on to invention of your own methods. When you study these quilts, you will be aware that the discipline of traditional forms can be combined with innovative ways of using and creating texture in the fabrics. Try using these ideas for your own approach to creative expression.

Klara Atalla,
Glitter/Splinter.
2 × 30 inches

Randomly shaped pieces of hand-woven silk have been applied to a foundation with machine satin stitch. The network of fine seams combined with the directional weave of the fabric create an interesting surface texture which has been contained by the dark border.

Rita Ball,
Cornwall, My County.
0 × 50 inches

A composition of squares in delicate pastels evokes the hazy colors of summer. To achieve the subtle gradations, the fabrics are all hand-dyed and the quilt is machine-pieced. The quilting designs, worked by hand, include contours, shells and curves which enhance the overall effect.

Gill Turley,
Sea and Strata.
51 × 28 inches

An adaptation of the "Log Cabin" and strip-piecing techniques are used in this impressionistic view of the seabed. The rock-like texture of the fawn fabric and its directional use blend well with the range of grays used in the upper part of the quilt. The dark outer border contains and serves to formalize the image.

Mary Fogg,
Fabric Roll.
50 × 54 inches

Strips of cotton and silk clever graded and stitched into this three-dimensional image complement the basic materia in use. Differences in the scale of the prints used serve to emphasize the solid-looking aspect of the quilt.

▼ **Gill Turley,**
Liberty Belle.
39 × 39 inches

Made as "an exercise using scrap triangles of fabric," this quilt illustrates well how effective subtle variations of tonal value can be. The different prints of these delicate fabrics seem to blend together, making the straight lines in the design shift before the eye. The smaller scale of the border pieces adds a finishing touch which complements the center well. The quilt is machine-pieced and hand-quilted.

Valerie Stevenson,
ever Not Prepared.
0 × 90 inches

his quilt, which was made to e a treasured heirloom, uses ppliqué and piecing techniques to display the maker's family coat of arms. Quilting designs done by hand and machine enhance the design and serve to illustrate Scottish/Irish links within the family.

▲ **Mrs A. Small,**
Egyptian Necklace.
24 × 24 inches

Inspired by the study of Ancient Egyptian art, this necklace made in gold and bronze lamé has rich surface decoration of machine-embroidery and -quilting. Each section of the necklace is made individually, then the pieces are joined with beads. This original piece of work makes effective use of both the fabrics and the techniques employed.

◀ **Louise Mabbs,**
African King Violet.
60 × 98 inches

The simplicity of each block combining plain and patterned fabrics is an ideal showcase for these African and Javanese batiks. Machine-piecing with some appliqué is combined with hand-quilting. The quilt is finished with a narrow patterned binding.

▶ **Kathleen E. Horner,**
Night and Day.
67 × 95 inches

Effective use is made of graded colors and values in this geometric machine-pieced interpretation of the "Night and Day" theme. A touch of realism is added by the appliquéd sun and moon and the hand-quilted sun rays. More hand-quilting is used on the border. The center panel is tie-quilted.

Agnete Kay,
y the Bow.
8 × 51 inches

n original quilt design, hand-
ieced from fabrics in fall
olors seen by the Bow river in
algary in Canada. This was
ade to celebrate "the
credible beauty of a
anadian fall."

◀ **Claudine Joho,**
Comédie.
87 × 75 inches

The allegorical theme of this
quilt is explained thus by the
maker: "The world always looks
different than it is. From the
outside shiny, from the inside
empty. Many people are like
this." Techniques used include
appliqué, machine-embroidery
and machine-quilting on hand-
dyed fabrics.

▶ **Frederike Kohlhaussen,**
Gewächse.
38 × 61 inches

Large and small-scale prints
are combined with plain fabrics
in a range of vibrant colors.
These work with the regularity
of the pattern on the quilt to
create a coherent surface.
Attention is at first focused on
the large prints, but the eye is
kept moving to identify regular
sequences of shape and color.
The whole design is contained
by a double border and a
narrow binding.

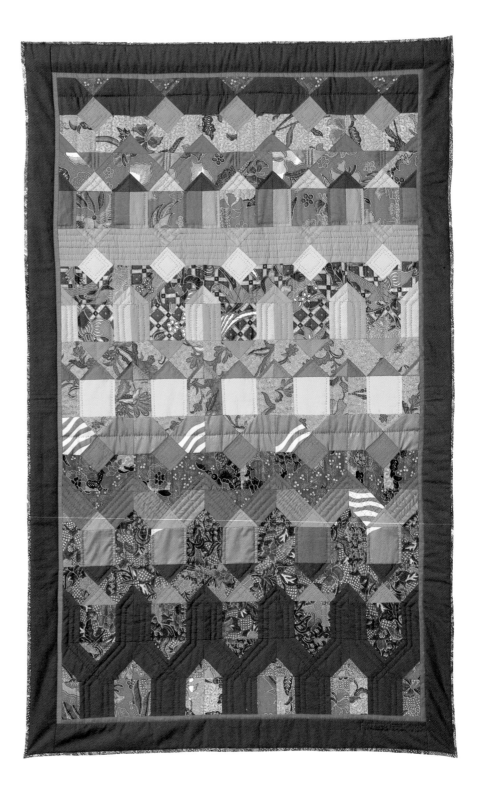

◀ **Carole Holland,**
Indigo Quilt.
96 × 60 inches

The simple composition of this
quilt is all that is needed to
show off the various decorative
indigo-dyeing methods used on
the fabrics. It is strip-pieced
and quilted by hand with
sashiko designs.

IMAGES

PICTORIAL QUILTS

Stitched pictures appear in many cultures and the idea of using fabric and thread to make images is found throughout the world. Banners and religious vestments were decorated with appliqué in medieval Europe, and in Nigeria large pictorial wall hangings are still made to record and celebrate events in a deceased person's life. Maori tribes of New Zealand and North American Indians traditionally decorate their clothing with pictures and symbols, and in Japan gold and silk are worked into elaborate appliqué panels.

The art involved in selecting the right fabric, composing the picture and stitching all the elements together, is illustrated by the quilts in this section. They display a range of approaches to fabric picture-making, and exhibit a variety of techniques.

Ingrid Wieland's *I. W. in New York* uses patchwork in a grid of squares and rectangles with skillfully graded fabric values. The difference in scale between the reflected self-portrait and the city skyline is startlingly effective. Irene McWilliam's *Events of 1990* uses the quilt form as a diary, to record events over one year. A personal viewpoint is forcibly expressed

in her choice of images. Records of happy events, favorite places and family celebrations can all be seen here. Another vivid personal message is portrayed by Natalia Manley in her quilt, *The Fabric of Life is Burning*. A range of techniques are used, and diverse fabrics, including silk, cotton, satin and polyester, are incorporated to dramatic effect. The combination of different textures is also employed by Magda Imregh in *Flower Valley* to recreate the landscape for which it is named. Eileen Costelloe's *Celebrations and Jubilations* conveys the exuberance of a party, while Jennie Lewis has perfectly described the view into an English country garden in *Through the Arched Window*. Momentary peace seems to reign in Rowena Reamonn's glimpse into the interior of a house in *Ten Minutes To Christmas*.

The addition of pieced patchwork to a fabric picture makes an effective border. Louise Bell uses this idea in both *Jungle* and *Quebec Scene*. A fabric already printed with a ready-made picture can also be used as part of a quilt. Katharine Guerrier's *Cat Crazy* is a humorous comment on how many people feel about their cats.

Jennie Lewis,
Through the Arched Window.
9 × 41 inches

Many different techniques are used in this view into a country garden, including English paper-piecing, appliqué, machine- and hand-embroidery, together with hand-painted and dyed fabric. The materials are also diverse: silk, net, organdie and cotton among them. This multiplicity of techniques and materials works together to create a pleasing image which is effectively contained by the padded frame.

Rowena Reamonn,
Ten Minutes To Christmas.
4 × 34 inches

A frozen moment in the life of a family is given as an intimate glimpse into the interiors of the house. Reverse machine-appliqué in cotton prints is combined with shadow-appliqué and embroidery. A flat synthetic batting was used.

▶ **Ann Fahl,**
Garden Wall.
47 × 40 inches

Personal observation of a favorite place seems to have inspired this quilt. The red brick wall is re-created in fabrics collected to reflect the color differences between the bricks, while the effect of the mortar is reproduced with gray and hand-dyed fabrics. Leaves, branches and vines are hand-appliquéd, and the tendrils are hand-embroidered. The free machine-quilting adds to the overall effect of the piece.

▶ **Fairfield Processing Corp. group quilt,**
The Circus Is Coming To Town.
65 × 80 inches

There is plenty of visual interest in each one of the blocks in this lively quilt which illustrates different aspects of the circus. Appliqué techniques are used in the blocks which are separated by sashing strips with corner squares.

◀ **Eileen Costelloe,**
Celebration and Jubilations.
68 × 53 inches

Made for an exhibition with the theme "Celebrations" to commemorate the tenth anniversary of the Irish Patchwork Society, this exuberant quilt depicting a box of fireworks is crazy patchwork "using a very free technique." Appliqué, quilting and embroidery are used with a collection of exotic materials such as silk, satin, brocade and lurex. The piece is made completely by machine.

▲ **Natalia Manley,**
The Fabric of Life is Burning.
54 × 60 inches

A quilt with a powerful message. In the maker's own words, "This quilt was inspired by the appalling waste of our Earth's resources. The back of the quilt is hand-painted in shades of black and gray to represent the burned-out forest." Machine-techniques include appliqué, quilting and embroidery on mixed fabrics, which include silk, cotton, satin and polyester.

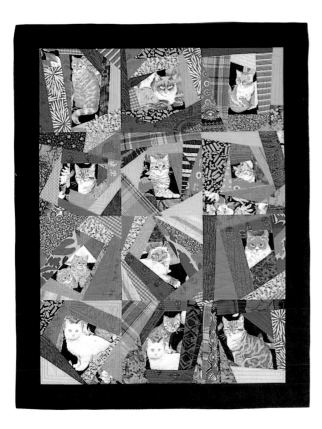

◀ Katharine Guerrier,
Cat Crazy.
36 × 29 inches

A novelty fabric printed all over with cats was the starting point for this quilt. Each block has a cut-out cat in the center and crazy shapes are added in rotation, stitched down onto a foundation in the machine crazy patchwork method. Blocks are joined edge to edge and the quilt has a black border finished with pieced straight binding. It is machine-quilted with different-colored thread in each block.

▼ Ann Fahl,
Flamingo Garden.
66 × 83 inches

Flamingo Garden is an elegant composition depicting flamingos in a fenced garden. Various techniques are used. The background is made of "freeform" patchwork, a term coined by the maker to describe her particular development of strip patchwork. "A lightweight fabric forms the foundation. On top, strips are sewn in a variety of ways to achieve interesting effects." The birds are machine-appliquéd, and the piece is embellished with beads and closely quilted.

▶ **Irene McWilliam,**
Events of 1990.
84 × 54 inches

A quilt made in the sampler block format in machine-appliqué. It depicts significant events over the period of one year. The maker compiles a file of newspaper cuttings which goes with the quilts (one has been made each year since 1986), and some of the squares, where appropriate, are autographed by the featured personality. This expands the tradition of those quilts made to commemorate events in a personal and graphic way. In addition to the events depicted on the blocks, more are listed around three edges of the quilt in free machine-writing, making this a record for future quilt historians to ponder over.

▲ **Ingrid Wieland,**
I. W. in New York.
108 × 58 inches

In a pieced view of the New York skyline, the large self-portrait is seen as a reflection in the side of one of the buildings. The restricted color scheme of blues, grays and black emphasizes the essential quality of the man-made environment.

◄ **Ingrid Wieland,**
Die Heilige Familie.
32 × 23 inches

This portrayal of the Nativity, done in a form of reverse appliqué, has a naive charm. The simplicity of the shapes and figures in the picture and the clear colors combine to retell this powerful story.

▶ **Ann Fahl,**
Winona Winter.
42 × 39 inches

An evocative quilt which makes use of a clever combination of techniques. The background is made of pieced triangles with overlays of sheer white voile. Icy white leaves are machine-appliquéd, as are the blue metallic willow leaves. Hand-beading with bugle beads adds further to the detail, and the piece is machine-quilted in jagged "icy" quilting.

◀ **Irene McWilliam,**
Butterflies.
19 × 22 inches

An abundance of butterflies flutter over luxuriant flowers in this garden fantasy. The flower bed is made from a collage of tiny, brightly colored pieces of fabric freely machine-stitched to the background. This provides a backdrop for the butterflies, themselves made from scraps of vibrant silks, cottons and polycottons and machine-appliquéd down. Further details are added with machine-embroidery. The edges are neatened and finished with piping.

Louise Bell,
Jungle.
0 × 60 inches

cat's jungle fantasy is gloriously depicted in this quilt. The shapes were freely drawn nd cut straight from the fabrics vith no preliminary sketches. he picture panel was built up nd stitched in progression sing machine satin stitch. The whole quilt has a layer of

batting but extra padding was added to some of the animals to give them a higher profile. Final details like the veins on the leaves and the silver cobweb were added to the picture with surface embroidery, by hand and machine. The patchwork border in multicolored "Sawtooth" strips with "Bear's Paw" corners is an appropriate finishing touch.

▼ **Louise Bell,**
Quebec Scene.
93 × 83 inches

An exhibition brief "Quebec and Indian art" sparked off the childhood memories which inspired this quilt. The maker, a native of Quebec, depicts the lake where she grew up, and has surrounded the picture with patchwork borders using

relevant block designs, including "Sawtooth," "Fir Trees," "Flying Geese," "Seminole," "Bear's Paw," "Log Cabin," and "Maple Leaf" designs. The piece is machine-appliquéd and machine pieced. Surface stitching is used to add final details to the picture, and the whole is machine-quilted.

◀ **Ann Fahl,**
Desert Palladian.
40 × 60 inches

In *Desert Palladian*, strip-piecing, cut and stitched together again, gives a painterly effect to the desert landscape in the background. The hand-appliquéd and beaded cactus flowers in the foreground (detail below) seem to emphasize the effect of distance created by the small pieces and flowing lines. Machine-quilting gives the quilt further textural detail.

Magda Imregh,
lower Valley.
6 × 24 inches

A picturesque valley carpeted with flowers in central Norway provided the inspiration for this quilt. A combination of different fabrics with various surfaces – cotton, silk, velvet and sateen – makes an interestingly textured landscape. The shapes are machine-appliquéd, and further details are added with hand embroidery and some hand-quilting.

▲ **Magda Imregh,**
Winter Pleasures.
9 × 12 inches

The character in a child's story is the starting point for this miniature quilt. It is made with cotton, silk and velvet, with some hand-painting on the cabin. The fabrics are machine-appliquéd, hand-embroidered and -quilted to create the dramatic snowscape.

INDEX

Note: page numbers in *italics* indicate illustrations

ACKNOWLEDGMENTS

The author and publisher would like to
thank the quilters who contributed work to
this book.